HELPING HEAVEN HAPPEN

HELPING
HEAVEN
HAPPEN

THINK YOUR WAY TO A BETTER LIFE

Donald Curtis

SAMUEL WEISER, INC.

York Beach, Maine

First published in 1992 by
Samuel Weiser, Inc.
Box 612
York Beach, ME 03910

Library of Congress Cataloging-in-Publication Data

Curtis, Donald.
    Helping heaven happen / by Donald Curtis.
      p. cm.
    Includes bibliographical references.
    1. New thought.   I Title.
  BF639.C8843   1992
  248.4'8997—dc20   92-1760
                                  CIP

ISBN 0-87728-759-7
MV

Cover illustration copyright © 1992 Kurt Pilz. Used by kind
permission of the Walter Holl Agency, Germany.

Printed in the United States of America

The paper used in this publication meets the minimum requirements of the American National Standard for Permanence of
Paper for Printed Library Materials Z39.48-1984.

Heaven Bound

We travel through a blackened sky,
Traversing level after level of
Permeating prisms of
Catalytic light patterns.
Brilliant color and sound
Penetrate and collect
Around our airy thoughts
That glide and soar by,
Freely reminiscent of wind.
Free At Last!

Spiritual freedom and mental focus
Are a perfect union for travel
To unmanifested realms of
Light and Beauty,
Soaring on, reaching new
Plateaus of universal delights.
At Long Last Free!

—Donald Curtis

TABLE OF CONTENTS

Foreword

The title of Dr. Donald Curtis' new book, *Helping Heaven Happen,* is so catchy and inviting that it makes you smile when you say it aloud. But the message of the book, though simply stated, is complex, profound, and deeply challenging.

In this sensitive, mind-stretching book, Dr. Curtis in a fresh and arresting way, shows you how — with divine help — you can retool your mind and heart, expand your consciousness, and remake your personal world by affirmative thought.

Here is a very practical text that offers concrete and specific guidelines for building a personal program of spiritual development for anyone attempting to achieve such a goal. Dr. Curtis personally leads you through a series of beautiful prayers of affirmation, meditation, and consciousness expansion entitled, "Personal Realization," at the end of each of the book's twelve chapters. This is an important feature for those in search of direct and immediate guidance and help. As you read these self-help prayers a number of times, meditating on them deeply and letting them really sink in, giving them the time to infuse your inner heart and mind to the very core of your God-centered spirit, you will actually — miraculously — experience that self-realization he promises.

This renowned spiritual teacher writes with the sureness of one who knows from experience that what he advocates will work because he, himself, has experienced it working in his own life and has witnessed it in the lives of many others who have turned to him for help.

This how-to-do-it spiritual guidebook, *Helping Heaven Happen* is, in part, also a revealing and moving memoir. This is one of the book's greatest charms. Donald Curtis' life experiences as a western farm boy, as an aspiring author, college speech instructor, university theater director, network radio performer, Broadway stage actor, and rising young movie star all serve as colorful parables to illustrate his illuminating teachings.

It was during these risk-filled, precarious years that he slowly learned the hard way that "your strength is only in your use of God's strength." Not in a blinding flash, but very gradually, he came to understand the ultimate truth that, when you really surrender your personal self totally to God's guidance and help through prayer, through meditation, and through concentrated thought in your daily living, your self becomes quite a different being from the ego it previously was — and all sorts of beautiful things begin to happen to you — and all kinds of glorious solutions result!

It was after this awakening of his own inner God-centered spirit, inspired by such notable spiritual teachers as Dr. Ernest Holmes and Dr. Manly Palmer Hall, that he was impelled to become a teacher and a minister of the gospel of love, as exemplified in the New Age teachings of the Church of Religious Science and the Unity School of Christianity.

Dr. Curtis served for many years as Senior Minister of the Unity Church of Dallas, and has often been a guest speaker for many other congregations and groups throughout the world. He is heard and seen regularly on radio and television with his message of abundant living. His work also includes service to humanity and global dedication to the service of God.

Dr. Curtis' insightful personal recollections greatly enrich his inspiring book. He unsparingly notes his own very human errors, during his earlier aspiring years, with a disarming frankness and a rare humility that is warmly appealing. Somehow he makes you feel that if he, despite his errors, managed to find the purpose and fulfillment of the life that God has now granted him, *surely you can do likewise!*

Dr. Curtis, however, is not writing an autobiography and, indeed, these personal stories—though fascinating—constitute only a small portion of his text. As he explains quite simply and modestly, "I have set forth my personal experiences merely as a metaphor for larger and more important concepts to show how these principles work. In the final analysis, what happens to any one of us is only important insofar as it contributes to all of us. The exchange of our individual experiences may well be the means by which we learn from each other, and move together to make a better world."

This is a wide-ranging, broad-gauged book directed toward people of all faiths who believe in the power of love and the divinity of life as well as its divine diversity.

Having known Dr. Curtis as a warm and wonderful friend for many years, I can assure you that he has no illusions about walking above water except when the deck of a sound ship is beneath his feet. The God-driven, God-inspired author of this impressive book would be the first to admit that he is just another vulnerable human being like the rest of us foot-dragging mortals. But I have also witnessed his growth into one of God's most selfless "tillers of the vineyard" and have seen him become—truly—one of God's great gentlemen. I'm proud to record that, by the practice of what he preaches, he is a living example of the self-development through divine surrender and cosmic consciousness that he dares us to emulate.

David Hyatt, Ph.D.[1]
San Francisco, California

---

[1]Dr. David Hyatt (1916–1992), a lifelong friend of the author, recently passed away. At the time of his death, he was President Emeritus, National Conference of Christians and Jews and International Council of Christians and Jews. Dr. Curtis is honored and grateful that Dr. Hyatt contributed this thoughtful foreword to the book.

PREFACE

During the years since the publication of my first book, *Your Thoughts Can Change Your Life,* a whole generation of people have changed their lives by applying the simple mental and spiritual techniques in that book and in the more than twenty others I have written following it.

This current volume will provide an update of what I know about this subject, and at least a partial record of how my thoughts have changed my own life, as well as reports of others who have made the same discovery. In *Your Thoughts Can Change Your Life* and my other books, I have set forth many techniques to help us change our lives by changing our thoughts. Life is a "do-it-yourself" proposition. There is nothing we cannot do, nothing we cannot be, no problem we cannot solve, no challenge we cannot meet if we take charge of our own thought processes.

As you build your own consciousness with affirmative thoughts, balanced emotions, and high spiritual awareness, you will be the person you want to be, and you will live the life you want to live.

This book is about you. It tells you everything you always wanted to know about yourself and may have been afraid to ask, or to do anything about. Here is something to help you meet that situation—so, read on!

Donald Curtis
Desert Hot Springs,
California, 1992

CHAPTER 1

IT'S UP TO YOU!

"If it is to be, it's up to me." Untold numbers of money clips, plaques, and cards are imprinted with this simple message. Many people use it as a motivational reminder to keep their minds focused upon the first step of accomplishing anything: Take charge of your own life!

The bottom line is that you cannot depend upon anyone to do anything for you. You shouldn't. You need the experience of doing things for yourself in order to gain strength, and resourcefulness. You are the only person you can depend upon, so start right now to rely upon yourself and yourself only. Oh, of course, others can and do help you in many ways, but they can't do it for you. What you do is your own specific personal domain. Don't let anyone take it away from you.

You are here in this life to live, to love, to learn, and to grow! These are all intensely personal areas. There is no one like you. There is much to be done that only you can do. Find out what it is, go all the way with it, and you will fulfill your reason for being.

Discover your own uniqueness and be true to it. Learn who you are, what you can do, and why you are here. Someone once said that if any two of us were just alike, one of us would be superfluous. Certainly you don't want to volunteer for that dubious honor. Be you, and everything else will fall into place.

There is nothing you cannot be, nothing you cannot do. There is no place where you leave off and God begins; there is no place where God leaves off and you begin. God made you in the image of Himself. God, thinking within Himself, upon Himself, about Himself, created the manifest universe — including you. And you can do the same. Create your own universe. Create your own world. Create your own life. Whatever it takes to make *you,* do it!

Create yourself! You are consciousness, which is made up of your thoughts, feelings, ideas, attitudes, concepts, dreams, and spiritual awareness. Formulate your self-concept and your self-image within your own mind. *Think about it and you will become it* is an unfailing law of the universe. Knowing it is more precious than diamonds, rubies or gold. It is the Pearl of Great Price.

Once you know who you are and where you are going, there is no limit to what you can do and accomplish. The world is your oyster! The kingdom of total being is yours, as well as everything in it! The creative process of the universe is flowing through your consciousness. You will never doubt or waver. You are in charge of your own life.

Once you realize that you are important and that you have a purpose in life, you will turn all your energies and attention toward doing all that you can, the best that you can.

Affirm: *I anticipate all impending events with enthusiasm and expectation of good.* This "turns me on" as I start each day, and as I embark upon any task or project. I found out long ago that once I make up my mind to do something, and have faith that I can do it, I get it done. Once I make a decision, get all doubts and procrastination out of the way, and take charge of myself, my life, and the innumerable situations before me, there is something greater than I am that works through me. This principle works for everyone. The only requirement is that you make up your mind about what you are going to do, and then do it.

Your Thoughts Can Change Your Life,[1] my first major book, was published in 1961, and has been a best seller in the inspirational and motivational field ever since. It took me a long time to get around to writing it, even though writing a book was one of my major goals since childhood. I looked with awe upon anyone who had written a book and would follow him around like a puppy dog, longing to be such an exalted being. I did a lot of fantasizing, but I never wrote a book.

This went on into my adult professional life. I continued to want to write a book; I planned to, but I never did. I wrote a lot in connection with my professions as teacher, college professor, and minister—even as an actor in Hollywood and on Broadway. But I never wrote a book, even though I had a great desire to do so.

I was always going around saying, "I've got to write a book. I've got to write a book!"

One day as I was counseling with Manly Palmer Hall, founder of the Philosophical Research Society in Los Angeles, where I was minister of the famed Science of Mind Church, I said to him, "I've got to write a book."

Mr. Hall, who himself had written well over 100 books, exclaimed, "Well, for goodness sake, why don't you go home and write one?"

I had never thought of that! I had never realized that the first thing I had to do to be a writer was to write a book! I was always in the process of making elaborate preparations: scribbling notes, constructing outlines, and amassing voluminous files of transcripts of the sermons, lectures, broadcasts, and classes I gave in my capacity as a minister and motivational speaker—but I had never sat down to write a book.

---

[1]See the appendix, page 238, for other books by the author.

I was always too busy—I had too many responsibilities—too much work to do and not enough time. Actually, I had too many excuses, all of which were true, but none of which was valid. They were appearances, but they were not reality. They had hypnotized me into believing that I had too much to do to write a book. I had let these appearances take charge of my life!

So I decided to change all of that; I decided to take charge of my own life. I decided to write a book! And the moment I made the decision, things started to happen. True Boardman, editor of the trade division of Prentice-Hall, contacted me to inquire whether I would be interested in writing a book for them, thus dispelling my false belief of many years that it was difficult to get a book published. (Of course it is if you don't write one!) But once you make your decision and take charge of your thoughts, feelings, attitudes, and actions, everything falls into place. Mighty forces are at your command.

To make a long story short, I bought a carton of #2 lead pencils and a ream of yellow paper, applied the seat of my pants to the seat of the chair, and started to work. *Your Thoughts Can Change Your Life* was finished in three and a half months.

Where did I get the time? I simply took charge of my life. I realized that time is an arbitrary illusion anyway—another false belief. I had all the time there is. The only time is now! In making the decision to get the book written, I resolved to use my time differently, more efficiently, to make time start serving me. I began getting up earlier each morning so I could write for several hours before taking up my duties as minister of the large Science of Mind Church.

In taking charge of my life, I set up a rigid, airtight schedule in order to get the book done as I had set out to do. In the process, I discovered that by managing my time and my life instead of letting them manage me, I had time and energy to do whatever needed to be done. My health improved; the quality of my work at the church improved.

Also I was able to write a book that has changed the lives of thousands of people all over the world, and has been a significant influence in the field of inspirational, motivational, and practical New Thought spiritual literature and teaching. People in many fields of endeavor, including business and professional people, teachers and ministers, continue to tell me how much *Your Thoughts Can Change Your Life* has changed their lives.

After many editions, the book sells more copies now, thirty years later, than it did when it was first published. This simply proves that the basic principles of decision, dominion, and high self-esteem are timeless, powerful factors in our lives when we activate them.

The purpose of this book is to inspire and instruct you in the process of establishing dominion over yourself and taking charge of your own life. It's up to you! The process entails five definite steps: 1) decision, 2) discipline, 3) dedication, 4) devotion, 5) determination.

DECISION

Decide right now that you can be whatever you want to be, and do whatever you want to do. Set your goals, establish your priorities, and do what you need to do. It is really quite simple, but essential, and is unbelievably powerful and productive when this process is followed:

1) Get your goals clearly in mind.	(Thinking Step)	Thought
2) Develop a strong conviction.	(Responding Step)	Feeling
3) Do everything you can.	(Working Step)	Action
4) Forget it, and let it happen.	(Releasing Step)	Acceptance

DISCIPLINE

As you take charge of your own life, you will be filled with a tremendous sense of purpose, which will lead you to develop physical, emotional, mental, and spiritual disciplines that keep you integrated as a whole person.

Physical Discipline: Keep your body in tune through proper diet, rest, and exercise. Your body is the servant of your consciousness and needs to be taken care of. Your body was made to serve your purposes, and will last as long as you need it—if you take care of it. If you don't, it will become a burden of disease, pain, and debilitation, holding you back instead of serving you. So, discipline yourself to take care of your body, and discipline your body to serve your will.

Emotional Discipline: It is most important to discipline your feeling nature because it is your power mechanism. Your feelings, attitudes, urges, and desires must be strictly controlled. They can never be allowed to run away with you. You must stand careful guard over your feelings. Keep all negativity out of your belief system by aligning your feelings with all that is positive and constructive.[2] Not only your thoughts but your feelings change your life. So, discipline them!

Mental Discipline: What you think determines what you are, what you become, and what results you achieve as your life unfolds. In developing your mental discipline, follow the same techniques as in developing emotional discipline. The same procedure applies to both. Thought and feeling must be perfectly coordinated in positive conviction. Only then can you achieve your full potential. If you think one thing but feel

---

[2]The reader is referred to four of my major books for more information on this subject: *Your Thoughts Can Change Your Life; Human Problems and How to Solve Them; Daily Power for Joyful Living; Science of Mind in Daily Living.* See the appendix for more information on how to obtain these publications.

another, the feeling will win. If you think success but feel failure, you will fail. The need to control your thoughts is obvious. You can discipline your mind to control the way you feel.

Spiritual Discipline: There is a still higher power which has dominion over both your thoughts and your feelings, and is the determining factor in building a whole consciousness. Your consciousness is the sum total of your thoughts, feelings, and spiritual awareness. A spiritual positive always overcomes a mental, emotional, physical, or experiential negative. You are spirit. You are not just a human being trying to make it in this world. You are a spiritual being going through a human experience on the way toward complete unfoldment of your real self.

Spiritual discipline is established and maintained through the regular practice of meditation. Meditation is the process of becoming still, releasing the thoughts and the senses from any concern with the outer, and focusing the entire attention upon contact with, and perception and awareness of, the reality within—the one source from which all things flow. Meditation consists of regular periods of living on the inner instead of the outer. Then, when your attention returns to the outer, the inner power flows through your consciousness, integrates all aspects of your being, and heightens your effectiveness. Meditation techniques have been used since ancient times by all those who have practiced personal spiritual disciplines. It is an important requirement in taking charge of your own life.

Find out about meditation. Much has been taught and written about it, including several of my books.[3] Develop your own meditation techniques and practice them faithfully. Meditation is the key to personal spiritual discipline.

---

[3]The reader is referred to *Daily Power for Joyful Living; Master Meditations; Forty Steps to Self-Mastery.* See the appendix for more information on how to obtain these publications.

DEDICATION

Dedicate your life to noble purpose and high ideals. Realize that you are here in this life to live, to learn, to love, and to serve. Dedicate yourself wholeheartedly to making the most of yourself that you possibly can and to helping other people as much as you can. Develop your powers and make the most of them. You are absolutely unique. There is something that you can do better than anything else; there is something that you can do that no one else can do. Find out what that is and do it! Unless you do, that part of creation will be left undone. That part of nature will be left unexpressed. That part of life will not be lived.

Dedicate yourself to being a whole person—physically, emotionally, mentally, and spiritually. Dedicate yourself to being the best person you can possibly be. Dedicate yourself to achievement. Hitch your wagon to a star!

Dedicate yourself to making the world a better place in which to live. Dedicate yourself to peace. Dedicate yourself to attaining and giving harmony and happiness. Dedicate yourself to overcoming your selfish false ego so that you may always express your higher self. The measure of your dedication determines the measure of your life.

DEVOTION

Devotion is that quality of character and consciousness that lifts your life to a higher octave. Devotion gives everything that you are and do expanded perception and awareness. Devotion is closely aligned with the true meaning of worship, which means *to make worthy.* However, devotion does not necessarily have anything to do with formal or organized religion, which is often more concerned with the *letter* and the form than it is the *spirit* and the essence. "For the letter killeth, but the spirit giveth life."[4]

---

[4]II Corinthians 3:6, Holy Bible, King James Version. All subsequent biblical references will be made in the text and will be to this edition.

You do not need to be a "religious" person per se, even though we are all more religious (or spiritual) than we realize. The word *religion* means *to bind back* (to the source), in other words, to unite the individual with the universal. This is a constant human need.

Devotion is the heart center of personal religion. It has always existed, and continues to be the major motivating force in men's lives, whether they know it or not. This ancient prayer is a paean of devotion:

> Oh Thou!
> Who give sustenance to the Universe
> From whom all things proceed,
> And to whom all things return,
> Unveil to us the face of the true spiritual Sun
> Hidden by a disc of golden light,
> That we may know the Truth
> And do our whole duty
> As we journey
> To Thy sacred feet.[5]

Devotion to the larger scope of things gives us the framework within which we live and move and have our being. Devotion gives meaning and purpose to our lives. Devotion is based upon belief in and love for a Supreme Being or Universal Intelligence, in Whose image and likeness we are made, and from which all creation flows. In other words, every one of us needs this consciousness of oneness which makes us whole. Weigh and consider this most important aspect of your life. Do not ignore it or neglect it. Without it, the true potential of your life cannot be achieved. With it, you will have a focal point of purpose and meaning that will flavor everything you do. Devotion to the infinite inner is the source

---

[5]T. Saraydarian, *Five Great Mantrams of the New Age* (Sedona, AZ: Aquarian Educational Group, 1975), p. 6.

of health, happiness, prosperity, success, and fulfillment. It is the supreme gift.

The activation of this magnificent component of your personal being is up to you. No one can achieve it or experience it for you. It is a path you must travel alone. But you will find that once you devote yourself to it, everything that happens—all experience—assists you in your quest. Find a balance in your life between the inner and the outer. Explore what the great idealistic philosophers, mystics, and teachers have said about this. Jesus said, "Neither shall they say, Lo here! or lo there! for behold, the kingdom of God is within you" (Luke 17:21).

Again, may I remind you that these instructions do not require an adherence to the formal religions of creed, denomination, or theology. They are psychological and philosophical concepts of spiritual truth, available to everyone in or out of churches, synagogues, mosques, or temples. Knowing this will free you for your own personal pattern of devotion.

The path will lead you to two specific areas of contemplation and awareness: 1) the universal, and 2) the individual presence of the universal within you. The universal is designated as "God" (or by whatever name God is called in other religious traditions). The individual presence in the Western (usually Christian) tradition is designated as "Christ." Focus your devotion upon these two realities and your destiny is sure to be fulfilled. It is up to you.

Your quest is a highly individual matter. God (Life) is everywhere. Find It in nature. Find It in other people, find It in everything you do. The great teachings of those who have gone before will help. Your quest and your devotion to it may lead you to participation in church worship (especially modern New Age, New Thought approaches), but not necessarily so. Music, art, opera, drama, and dance may be the gates by which you enter the great realm. Poets, mystics, and teachers may be found to walk with you along the way, but in the final analysis you must find the way yourself through decision, discipline, dedication, devotion, and determination.

As you grow in awareness of the larger scope of things, you will experience a growing realization that inner space is much more vast, but at the same time much more imminent, than outer space. You will realize that the divine presence (God individualized) is the Christ—your own higher self. When this realization comes, your devotion will be permanent. The major essence of your life will be focused equally upon God (the universal) and Christ (its individualization within you).

DETERMINATION

The fifth step in this magnificent and adventurous journey of life is your own personal determination to be a winner; to accomplish whatever it is that is given you to do. As the Bible instructs, "Whatsoever thy hand findeth to do, do it with all thy might" (Ecclesiastes 9:10).

You are never confronted with anything you cannot handle. You are capable of solving, doing, and conquering anything and everything that comes your way. You have the seeds of greatness within you; you are God in action. There is nowhere God leaves off and you begin. Mighty forces are at your command. Learn to use them wisely and well.

This will undoubtedly entail a series of experiences that will eventually make you realize that there is more to this business of life than personal ego gratification. A strong, healthy personal life and will are important for true achievement, but the achievement must have a higher purpose than just fulfilling your personal desires. Total good must come from your efforts, otherwise they are in vain. Jesus said, "Let your light so shine before men, that they may see your good works, and glorify thy father which is in heaven" (Matthew 5:16).

Realization of your place in the larger scheme of things will eventually come to you. You may, as I did—and often still do—need to recognize that there is much more to life than personal achievement and gratification. Personal will and ambition are necessary, but only as the means for providing the dynamic through which the will of God (Good) may be done through you.

It is essential to maintain balance and order in our lives. Habits formed in childhood are deeply rooted and often take real discipline and determination to change. I came from a farm background and was conditioned in a very strict work ethic. I had a wonderful father and mother—loving, good, honest, responsible, and deeply religious—but they were conditioned by the belief that life is a struggle, and that hard work is the only way to achievement, recognition, and accomplishment. Does this sound familiar to you? It is not all bad in itself, but it can lead to a lot of pain, frustration, needless unnecessary suffering, and sometimes bitterness and disappointment.

I tried to fit into this background by working hard, but even as a small boy, I was aware that all of the struggle and hard work brought virtually no happiness or self-esteem to my parents. They did not complain, because this was the only life they knew, and they led me to believe that it would be the same for me.

I rebelled inwardly against this limitation upon my life. I developed a strong determination within myself that I was going to do great things in the world. I developed an abrasive aggressiveness as I pursued my goals. I let nothing deter me from what I was determined to do. I overcompensated for my feelings of inferiority by becoming an overachiever, although I didn't achieve nearly as much as many of my contemporaries. My brother, who did not subject himself to the inner drive that I did, went about his own quiet path of accomplishment another way and usually succeeded far more often than I did, despite all of my efforts.

However, as this chapter indicates, your life is a matter of self-determination. No one can live for you, love for you, grow for you, or learn your lessons for you. Life is a school, and every lesson must be learned. As you travel up the mountain, the important thing to realize is that all roads lead to the summit, and we all eventually make it. One thing is certain, however: you do not accomplish it by yourself. It is important that you follow these five steps, but it is important, too, that you realize you are not alone on your journey. Consider these assurances from the Bible:

"Your Father knoweth what things ye have need of before ye ask him." (Matthew 6:8)

"It is the Father's good pleasure to give you the kingdom." (Luke 12:32)

"He performeth the thing that is appointed for me." (Job 23:14)

"The Lord will perfect that which concerneth me." (Psalms 138:8)

Determine to go all the way. Keep moving inward, onward, and upward. Keep your eye on the mountain top. Let nothing deter you from your avowed purpose. Have confidence in yourself and faith in that within you that is greater than you are. Remember, that which is within you is greater than that which is in the world. Jesus was speaking about you and me when He said, "In the world ye shall have tribulation, but be of good cheer; I have overcome the world" (John 16:33).

Trust in yourself. Take charge of your own life. Make your own decisions. Think well of yourself. Have the courage of your convictions. Set your goals. Establish your priorities. Take one step at a time, one after another. This is the first day of the rest of your life. This is the best of all possible worlds. Your opportunity for life achievement is greater than anyone has ever known. "Press toward the mark of the prize" (Philippians 3:14). It's up to you!

Personal Realization

Thank you, Father-Mother God, for the abundance which is mine. Thank You for my life and the privilege of living it. Thank You for my unlimited potential. Thank You for my mind, heart, soul, and body. Thank You for Infinite Intelligence individualized in me. Thank You for the Divine Presence dwelling within me. Thank You for the emergence of my Higher Self. Thank You for the lessons of life and my ability to learn them.

Thank You for my unlimited potential and the faith that I will fully express it. Thank You for my realization of the meaning and purpose of life, and the capacity to live it fully.

The free, full flow of life is surging through me, making me whole on every level. I am an integrated being, spiritually, mentally, emotionally, physically, and in my world of activity and expression. I am alive, alert, awake, and attuned. The Infinite is temporized in me. The Universal is individualized in me. Unlimited love is expressed through me. Strong and steadfast faith is embodied in me. I am aware of my purpose and life, and I pursue it relentlessly and joyously.

I dwell in a timeless, unconditioned Universe of infinite inner and outer space. I am a good steward. I take good care of my many gifts, abilities, opportunities and responsibilities. I develop them and express them for the glory of God and in service to all mankind. I make my own decisions under inner guidance and direction, and I abide by them as I apply myself toward fulfilling them, correcting my mistakes, and learning the lessons which I encounter.

I am disciplined in every aspect of my life. I am in charge of my thoughts, feelings, and actions. I surrender my will to the Higher Will. I am a disciplined individual.

I am dedicated to the good, the true, and the beautiful. I am dedicated to noble purpose and high ideals. I am a dedicated being.

I am devoted to the all-benevolent Oneness and Wholeness which we call God. I am devoted to the perfect, shining individualized Light which is the Christ. I am a devoted soul.

I am determined to reach the summit of the mountain. I am determined to be a credit to God and to myself. I am determined to do all I can to help others. I am a determined person.

Thank You, Father-Mother God, for the realization that all of this is up to me. And so it is.

CHAPTER 2

THE GLASS IS ALWAYS HALF FULL

A glass of water can be in one of three states: it can be full, it can be empty, or it can be at some level in between. There are two points of perspective for a partially filled glass. A person of a predominantly negative consciousness would say, "The glass is half empty." The person with a positive, enthusiastic, optimistic consciousness says, "The glass is half full."

These are two basic approaches to life. Each produces the results which come about in that person's life—further confirmation that your thoughts determine what happens in your life.

Many anecdotes illustrate the difference between the positive and negative individual—between the optimist and pessimist: the joyous person awakens each morning exclaiming, "Thank You, God, another day!" while the dour individual moans, "Oh, God! Another day!"

The pessimist twin could only complain about the pile of hay he had to stack in the barn. His optimist brother exclaimed joyously, "With all this hay around here, there's bound to be a pony somewhere!"

Which twin are you? Optimism and pessimism are habitual states of mind. They are both formed by your approach to life through your thoughts, feelings, and attitudes. Even though some of your experiences, failures, and frustrations may tend to make you negative, fearful, and discouraged, you cannot afford to let that happen. Take control, renew your thoughts, and align them positively and constructively, thereby creating a channel for success.

THE STRUCTURE OF YOUR MIND

The experiences of your life are determined by the polarity of your thought. A simple explanation of the structure of your mind and how it works will help you understand how your thoughts determine your experience. There are three levels of

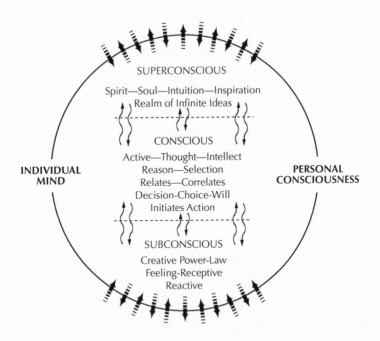

Figure 1. The three levels of the mind.

mind: the superconscious, the conscious, and the subconscious, as shown in figure 1.

Your conscious mind receives ideas from the superconscious, and formulates them into concepts, thoughts, plans, and choices, initiating creative action by impressing them upon the subconscious mind, which receives them and brings them into manifestation. Thus, the superconscious is the realm of ideas; the conscious chooses, selects, and initiates action; the subconscious receives the impress of your thoughts and acts upon them.

This brief explanation will help you understand why and how your thoughts change your life. It is obvious that high-level affirmative thought produces superior experience. Check yourself out by asking yourself four basic questions:

1) Do I have an affirmative attitude toward life?

2) Do I have a philosophy fit to live by?

3) Do I have a self fit to live with?

4) Do I have a world fit to live in?

AN AFFIRMATIVE ATTITUDE TOWARD LIFE

Attitude is everything. You can if you think you can. If you don't think you can, you can't. It's as simple as that. Always see the glass half full. Give everything, including yourself, the benefit of the doubt. Expect the best and the best will come to you. Develop an optimistic, upbeat attitude toward life. Be enthusiastic about everything. Continue to use this affirmation: *I anticipate all impending events with enthusiasm and expectation of good.*

One day a young man came to me for spiritual and mental reinforcement in securing regular employment in his chosen field. He had been terminated from his previous position and had been unemployed for nearly six months. He had been interviewed many times, but was never hired. He always lost out at the last minute. Understandably, he had become desperate and discouraged.

Now he had another opportunity. A position that was exactly what he wanted had turned up. He had already had his final interview, and the prospective employer had promised to let him know something soon. When he came to see me, the call had not yet come, and he was filled with anxiety and fear that he had lost out again.

"It's no use!" he cried. "I know I'll never get it. They should have called me by now. What am I going to do?"

"Just a minute," I said, steadying him. "Let's not give up now. They probably haven't completely made up their minds yet. Let's help them do that."

"How?" he asked.

"By believing that you have the job," I replied.

"But I don't!" he exclaimed. "They haven't called me."

"That may be because you haven't been ready to receive the call."

"Oh, I'm ready!"

"Let's be sure. How would you feel if you got the call right now, telling you that you have the job?"

"Why, I would jump up and down with joy! I would thank God, and I would shout, 'I've got it! I've got it! Hallelujah, I've got it.'"

"All right, let's do that right now," I advised him. "Make yourself feel the way you will feel when the call comes that the job is yours."

"Okay! I get it," my friend replied. "You mean that my attitude of gratitude and joy will help cause them to hire me?"

"Of course! Let's try it!"

We became quiet for a moment, and then made several statements of affirmation that the desired good was already true, and that we awaited the good news with total confidence. The young man was at perfect peace when he left, because he had reached the realization that his desire was fulfilled. In a few hours, he called me with the news that the call had come and everything was settled. He was to begin work the next day. Everything worked out.

Now he shares with everyone the key to demonstration: Develop now the feeling you will have when the good you desire comes about. This principle is constantly at work as a major causative. Try it. You'll like it!

AN AFFIRMATIVE PHILOSOPHY OF LIFE

Your affirmative, joyous attitude must be real. You must really believe what you say. Fall in love with life and live it fully. Know that only good can come about in your life. Develop a strong inner consciousness that you can be whatever you want to be and do whatever you want to do. Adopt this overview of life:

Waiting

Serene, I fold my hands and wait,
 Nor care for wind nor tide nor sea;
I rave no more 'gainst time or fate,
 For lo! my own shall come to me.

I stay my haste, I make delays—
 For what avails this eager pace?
I stand amid the eternal ways
 And what is mine shall know my face.

Asleep, awake, by night or day,
 The friends I seek are seeking me,
No wind can drive my bark astray
 Nor change the tide of destiny.

What matter if I stand alone?
 I wait with joy the coming years;
My heart shall reap where it has sown,
 And garner up its fruit of tears.

The waters know their own, and draw
　　The brook that springs in yonder height;
So flows the good with equal law
　　Unto the soul of pure delight.

The stars come nightly to the sky;
　　The tidal wave unto the sea;
Nor time, nor space, nor deep, nor high,
　　Can keep my own away from me.[1]

This is only one of many poems and inspirational writings that will help you remember that the glass is always half full. The Bible is full of examples of men and women who triumphed over difficulty and came out winners. Many great novels and plays, as well as books on philosophy, psychology, inspiration, personal development, and success achievement, confirm the effectiveness of positive expectancy.

I have always had faith in myself, coupled with a bulldog tenacity and perseverance in doing what I wanted to do. Unfortunately, this was often characterized by too much aggressiveness, false ego projection, and self-centeredness. As a result, I often suffered setbacks, and was no stranger to feelings of discouragement. But throughout my life I have done what I wanted to do, achieved what I wanted to achieve, accomplished what I was supposed to accomplish, up to the point where I am now. And I feel that I have only begun. I know that I can go much further—not for any good that I seek or desire for myself, but to develop my full potential for the good of other people, the world, and the entire universe.

I sincerely believe that this is the only philosophy fit to live by. Emerson hits the nail on the head when he says that the purpose of life is to move better up to best.

You see, the dynamic of an affirmative philosophy gives you the energy, power, incentive, initiative, inspiration, deter-

---

[1] J. Burroughs, "Waiting" in *One Hundred and One Famous Poems* (Chicago, IL: The Cable Co., 1929).

mination, knowledge, and skill to fulfill your purpose in life. Have no doubt—the glass is always half full, on its way to being completely full.

You can achieve anything you want, if you want it badly enough, and fulfill the requirements for it. Your motivation and conviction are greater factors in your achievement than anything else. Consciousness is the only reality.

A Whole Self, Fit to Live With

As you release the dynamic of your affirmative, achiever consciousness, it is important that you develop integration and balance, spiritually, mentally, emotionally, and physically. Each of these areas is an important component of your self, your being. If there is too much concentration on any one of them, or on personal achievement alone, distortion develops. You will not be happy, you will have trouble getting along with yourself and others, and you will come nowhere near achieving your potential, no matter how capable you are or how hard you try.

You are a wonderful, beautiful organism. Keep your entire being in perfect working order. Develop your consciousness of yourself with uniqueness and individuality, as a spiritual being. This orientation will promote the integration and balance that are necessary for real achievement.

Early Confusion: There was a strange contradiction in the instruction I received from my father and mother. My mother would often tell me that I was very special and had great work to do. My father always admonished me to do better. But both of my parents somehow gave me the feeling that being a farm kid, I wasn't quite as good as a city kid. My father definitely had feelings of inferiority because he was "just a farmer," and my mother felt trapped and frustrated in the farm life, unable to develop the abilities she knew she had.

Even as a child, I could see and feel this confusion in consciousness around me. As much as I loved my parents, I did not want to be like them, and very early started to pursue the quest for my own goals and my own identity. I believed I had more ability than my father; there was no doubt in my mind that I was superior to others. I took no pains to hide my belief in my own superiority from anyone.

Doing farm work, I was often alone for long periods of time as I plowed the fields or herded cattle. I dreamed dreams; I visualized myself the monarch of all that I surveyed. I declared that I would never be a farmer, and was very outspoken about it. This offended my father, and even though he encouraged me to study hard, excel in school, get good grades, and go on to college, his advice was that I had better plan to be a farmer. This caused considerable conflict between us.

The Quest for Identity: I decided I would be an author. I thought then, and I still do, that writing is the acme of all human endeavor. The power of the spoken word is great, but it can only be given permanence and sustained by the power of the written word. As a boy, and all through my teens, I studied and read everything I could about writing, and I idolized writers. I took on the role of a romantic, imaginative author, dreaming up fantastic plots and glorious happenings as I plowed the fields and traveled the roads and rode the range.

My fantasies would come to an abrupt end when I returned to the barn with my saddle horse and started to tell my father about my dreams. He dismissed them abruptly by putting a shovel in my hands and telling me to get busy cleaning the stalls and stables.

My mother was more sympathetic and encouraging, but they were both puzzled and troubled by this strange, determined dreamer they had for a son. However, there was great love among my parents and siblings (a younger brother and two younger sisters) and me. There was always encouragement and pride in our accomplishments, which gave us all feelings of confidence and security.

Our schoolwork ranged from good to superior. While my brother achieved academic distinction, my achievements were in school government and extracurricular activities — the school paper, dramatics, and public speaking contests. I also participated in all athletics, but while capable, I was not outstanding.

New Directions: However, I did become outstanding in acting and speaking. I continued writing for school publications into college, but my concentration was in the other fields. Early in high school I was fortunate to be taught, encouraged, and inspired by Doris Marsolais, who directed the plays and coached me for speaking contests. I am eternally grateful for this early training, which led me to study speech and theater in college. At the same time, some of my favorite subjects were grammar, English usage, writing, and English literature.

Graduating from high school in the midst of the depression, I attended Eastern Washington College in my home town of Cheney, Washington, where I had the tutelage of two remarkable teachers who were both graduates of Northwestern University School of Speech: Mary Snyder, who taught dramatics, and Marie Hollingshead, who taught public speaking. Both recommended me for a scholarship at Northwestern during my second year.

I made plans to go there, even though my scholarship would only cover my tuition, and I would have to work for my board and room and all other expenses. I had no concern about that whatsoever. I had made up my mind to be an actor, and going to Northwestern seemed the first step.

I worked as much as I could, saving what I earned, because my father had made it clear that he could help me very little, since he and all the other farmers had been hard hit by the depression.

When my father saw me off on the train for Chicago, he gave me $100, and said, "Well, Son, since you're determined to do this thing, it's up to you from here on. You say you're going to be an actor. I don't know anything about that, and I don't think you do either. I understand it's a very tough business, and hard to make a living at. Just promise me one thing, that you will get your college education and teacher's credentials, and prepare yourself to make at least $200 a month, and I'll never have to worry about you."

I promised. It seems humorous now, in this day of inflated monetary values, but in the depression days, $200 was a respectable monthly salary expectancy for a college graduate. Through a lot of hard work and a continuing scholarship, I made it through Northwestern.

I wanted to be an actor in Hollywood or on Broadway more than ever, but as much confidence as I had in myself, those two places scared me. It was then, and still is, very difficult to make a living, let alone attain professional recognition, in Hollywood or on Broadway. So I decided to take my father's advice and teach.

I got a job as a speech instructor at Allegheny College for $200 a month. The next year, after I had completed my M.A. degree, I was Associate Professor of Speech and Drama at Duquesne University at not much more. However, I never gave up on my desire to be an actor, and through a series of events—including acting stints at the Pittsburgh Playhouse, the Cleveland Playhouse, and the famed Pasadena Playhouse—I eventually was put under contract in Hollywood, where I enjoyed a modest success for a number of years, followed by some seasons on Broadway and in radio and television.

Something Greater: However, by this time something greater had come into my life, and I phased out of show business and became a minister and metaphysical teacher and lecturer, which I have been for many years.

After a progression of unfoldment, spiritually, personally, and professionally, I became minister of the Unity Church of Dallas and was its senior minister for nearly twenty years.

The challenges of this large ministry were many and varied on all levels, but each one taught me lessons that are necessary for growth and effectiveness. Whatever I accomplished was the result of using the principles set forth in this book. My thoughts have changed my life and they continue to do so. This is true of everyone. It is true of you.

I have set forth my personal experiences in this chapter merely as a metaphor for larger and more important concepts to show how these principles work. In the final analysis, what happens to any single one of us is only important insofar as it contributes to all of us. The exchange of our individual experiences may well be the means by which we learn from each other and move forward together to make a better world.

A World Fit To Live In

I am dedicated to helping, teaching, healing, motivating, and inspiring all people. My expanded ministry is international and universal in scope. I am part of a vast network of New Age individuals and groups throughout the world who are serving together under the Hierarchy in bringing richer, fuller, more significant living to all people. As I travel around the globe, I join with many others in fellowship, study, and mutual identity with, and a commitment to, the Great Work of bringing about the kingdom of love, beauty, enlightenment and peace on earth.

Peace within the individual is the path to world peace. The matter of peace within the personal consciousness is so vital to individual and universal good that it requires further emphasis. Personal peaceful integration results in your having a good disposition, the sum total of all desirable thoughts, feelings, attitudes, and qualities. We might well say, "Your Disposition Can Change Your Life." There could be no truer statement.

Someone said of a friend, "George has a very even disposition—he's always mad." Of course, you are interested in the opposite—a kind and loving disposition. How shall you go about changing your disposition and building the kind you wish to have? Let's start with joy. The Bible says, "Weeping may endure for a night, but joy cometh in the morning" (Psalms 30:5).

But joy does not just come to you; you develop it within yourself. Joy is a soul quality. Gratitude, appreciation, participation and inspiration are all part of joy. Jesus said, "He who drinketh of the water that I shall give him shall have in him a well of water springing up into everlasting life" (John 4:14).

That just about describes what joy is. You can be as joyous as you want to be, even in the face of pain, problems, trouble, and adversity. See the glass half full, and you can go with Shakespeare into the Forest of Arden (Life) as he proclaims:

Sweet are the uses of adversity;
Which, like the toad, ugly and venomous,
Wears yet a precious jewel in his head;
And this our life, exempt from public haunt,
Finds tongues in trees, books in the running brooks,
Sermons in stones, and good in every thing.[2]

PERSONAL REALIZATION

My cup runneth over. I am filled to overflowing with joy and enthusiasm. Nothing is too good to be true. Nothing is too wonderful to happen. Life is a never-ending series of magnifi-

---

[2]W. Shakespeare, *As You Like It,* Act II, scene 1, ll. 12–17.

cent surprises for me. The abundant gifts of the Infinite flow into my experience.

I am an eternal optimist. I expect good, and good comes to me. I expect the best, and I always get it. I live, I love, I learn, and I sing with joy. Lightness and scintillating laughter bubble up from my soul. I am a happy person. I am a joyous person. I am filled with ecstasy as my heart, mind, and soul integrate and unify with the positive vibrations of the Cosmos itself. The entire Universe confirms the wonder and beauty of Total Being. I live forever, one day at a time. Each moment of my long, active, vital, eternal life is filled with the vibrations and essences of Eternity.

I am a native of Eternity. I am an individual expression of Divinity. I am alive, alert, awake, and enthusiastic. I am alive with the joy of life. There is nowhere God leaves off and I begin. I am One with Total Being.

Each moment is precious to me. I live my life fully, experiencing its potential on every level—spiritual, mental, emotional, physical, material—in my world of activity and worthy endeavor.

Thank You, Father-Mother God, for my life and the privilege of living it. Thank You for Love and the privilege of giving and receiving it. Thank You for Joy and the privilege of expressing it. Thank You for Peace and the privilege of experiencing it and sharing it with everyone everywhere.

Thank You for the Great Work and the privilege of doing it. Thank You forever, from now on. And so it is.

CHAPTER 3

BELIEVE IN YOURSELF!

When the Oracle at Delphi gave the instruction, "Man, know thyself," we can assume that it meant the Real Self—the True Self—the Whole Self. But in order to know yourself, in order to believe in yourself, it is necessary that you have a concept of what your "self" is. We are constantly talking about "myself," without really stopping to think about which self we are referring to. Your self can be thought of as a composite of these seven basic levels:

1) Universal Self ⎫
2) Spiritual Self   ⎬   (HIGHER SELF)
3) Soul Self   ⎭

4) Mental Self

5) Emotional Self ⎫
6) Physical Self   ⎬   (LOWER SELF)
7) Material Self   ⎭

You may be referring to any one or a combination of these selves when you say "myself," without being aware of what you actually mean. The self is very complex. Is it any wonder that we have difficulty understanding others, when we seldom even understand ourselves?

THE UNIVERSAL SELF

Free your mind from all tangible, external objective thoughts and let it expand into a new dimension of awareness. Do not limit or confine yourself to any conditioned concept whatsoever. Affirm: *I am an infinite being. I have always been, and always will be, beyond any concept of time or space. I am a child of the Universe; I am a being of Light; I am one with all that is. There is nowhere that the Universe leaves off and I begin. I live forever in the here and the now.*

Go over and over this paragraph, interspersing the affirmations with periods of silent realization, until you identify completely with this expanded concept of yourself. This Universal Self is the Reality of you. Know it. Accept it. Be ever aware of what you really are. Dwell constantly in this higher realm. Relate all other aspects of yourself to It, and realize that even though you function on several levels (selves) simultaneously, you are one being. You are One with God.

Forever Free

Timeless, endless, eternal continuum,
Of progressively unfolding awareness,
Building a consciousness unlimited by
Human, worldly, external concerns.

Immersed in the boundless essence of pure being,
Aligned with the celestial bodies,
Vibrating in rhythm with the Universe,
Enlivened by the energies of the Cosmos.

Together we enter the higher reaches of being,
Released from all earthly limitation,
Forever free in the limitless scope of eternity,
Together as one in God forever.

Rise above your humanity; ascend to your divinity. Affirm: *I am not just a human being trying to make it in this world. I am a Universal, Spiritual Being, living through a human experience, on the way toward complete and perfect unfoldment of my Real Self.* This universal thought will change your life more than you realize. Now, become aware of the other levels of your self that are within the Universal Self.

THE SPIRITUAL SELF

Now that you have accepted that you are much more than a one-dimensional human being, it is easier to clarify your concept of your self. The universal being with which you are identified and unified is individualized in you. You are a point of light within the great light. You are an individual expression of God. Affirm: *Wherever God is, I am.*

Become aware of your identity with the spirit as your "individuality," as distinguished from your "personality," which we will discuss later. This "individuality," this "point of Light within the Mind of God,"[1] is the Christ of your being—"the true Light that lighteth every man that cometh into the world" (John 1:9). Paul calls it, "Christ in you, the hope of glory" (Colossians 1:27). He says, "I live; yet not I, but Christ liveth in me" (Galatians 2:20); "I can do all things through Christ which strengtheneth me" (Philippians 4:13).

Be patient with yourself. Give yourself time to be comfortable with this concept of "the Christ." You will find that it adds dimension to your already established spiritual and religious beliefs, as well as giving you a point of spiritual reference if you are seeking spiritual understanding.

Marcus Bach once said in a public address that there comes a time in every person's life when his or her path crosses the Path of the Christ, and life changes from that time on. It has been true in my own life. I was reared with ortho-

---

[1] A. A. Bailey, *Ponder on This: A Compilation* (New York and London: Lucis, 1971), unnumbered frontmatter.

dox religious beliefs, including the traditional concept of Jesus Christ as a person. There is much more to it if one is to experience the full dimension of the Christ. This came to me through the teachings of the Science of Mind in the Church of Religious Science, from its founder, Dr. Ernest Holmes (I served as a Religious Science minister for nearly twenty years), and through the teachings of Unity, in which I have been a minister for over twenty years.

During this entire period, the unfoldment of my life and its effectiveness have been based upon my increasing awareness of myself as a spiritual being. The following affirmations, which I repeat regularly, have grown out of my own consciousness and strengthen my personal concept of my true being:

> *I am a point of Awareness within the Christ of God.*
> *I am a point of Being within the Soul of God.*
> *I am a point of Light within the Mind of God.*
> *I am a point of Love within the Heart of God.*
> *I am a point of Life within the Body of God.*
> *I am a point of Manifestation in the World of God.*
> *I am a point of Creativity within the Energy of God.*
> *I am a point of Vibration within the Action of God.*
> *I am a point of Joy within the Glory of God.*
> *I am a point of Beauty within the Perfection of God.*
> *Whatever God is, I am!*

Along with these affirmations, The Christ Prayer is a daily guide of commitment, dedication, and devotion. It is a point of focus for the Christ Teaching that is the foundation of my ministry and which has helped thousands identify with the Christ within themselves. Please make it your own:

The Christ Prayer

Oh Christ, Thou Son of God!
My own eternal Self!

Live Thou Thy Life in me.
Do Thou Thy Will in me.
Be Thou made Flesh in me.
I have no will but Thine.
I have no self but Thee.
Oh Christ, Thou Son of God![2]

THE SOUL SELF

Although "God" and "Spirit" and "Soul" are mysteries, they are not unknowable. We are admonished to know thyself, which is not possible unless we know something about the components of the whole self.

In the Biblical account of the Creation, we are told, ". . . the Lord God formed man of the dust of the ground, and breathed into his nostrils the breath of life; and man became a living soul" (Genesis 2:7).

The importance of the individual soul is stressed in many Biblical allusions to it. "For what is a man profited, if he shall gain the whole world, and lose his own soul?" (Matthew 16:26). More recently, one poet exclaimed:

Build thee more stately mansions, O my soul
    As the swift seasons roll!
    Leave thy low-vaulted past!
Let each new temple, nobler than the last,
Shut thee from heaven with a dome more vast,
    Till thou at length art free,
Leaving thine outgrown shell by life's unresting sea![3]

It is obvious that in the search for your own identity, your soul is an area of your being that you can do something

---

[2]Anonymous, in *Wings of Song* (Unity Village, MO: Unity School, 1984), p. 254.
[3]O. W. Holmes, "The Chambered Nautilus" in *One Hundred and One Famous Poems* (Chicago, IL: The Cable Co., 1929).

about. It is a primal, permanent, and eternal part of your complete self which has been created by the original, the first cause, but then has been given to you to develop and care for.

The universal individualizes in the spiritual, which conceptualizes in the soul. These three comprise the higher self. Your soul is developed to the degree that your mind sets itself the assignment of assisting in building and strengthening it. The Christ is your individuality—your true self.

Your soul is what you are at this point in time, at the level of spiritual awareness and understanding you have attained. As your mind dwells upon your spiritual nature, your soul reaches its full development. As your mind dwells upon your lower nature—the emotional, physical, and material— the development of your soul is impeded and delayed. In other words, your soul is what you are, but you determine what your soul is. In his teachings, Manly Palmer Hall suggests there are eight lessons of the soul.[4]

Grace: Grace is humility in the human realm. It is an attainable quality. Grace is the way God is; it is the impersonal outpouring of God's love into His creation. A person filled with grace is one who has learned that there is a higher level of personal unfoldment than human personality and human ego.

Peace: Put no limit on the peace you can enjoy within yourself, the peace you can bring into your family, into the organization where you work, into society as a whole. Each day when you awaken, make peace your number one priority. "Thou wilt keep him in perfect peace, whose mind is stayed on thee: because he trusteth in thee" (Isaiah 26:3).

Love: Learn to love the being within you—the reality beyond your human personality—your true individuality—the Christ

---

[4]These were given in oral teachings and in personal counselling.

within. Love is perhaps the greatest lesson of the soul. It is not something you put on like a garment. It must permeate every cell of your body, every vibration of your thought, and every aspiration of your soul.

Understanding: "Therefore get wisdom: and with all thy getting get understanding" (Proverbs 4:7). Understanding is "standing under" God's law. Krishnamurti says, "There are only two kinds of people in the world, those who know and those who don't."[5] It is essential to become one who knows; to know requires understanding, which demands discipline. When you accept this, your discipline becomes a joyous personal choice.

Gentleness: Your strength comes from within; your strength is your use of God's strength. The soft touch, the kind word, the loving, caring manner are all essentials of the gracious life. The gentle expression of strength and authority is much more becoming and effective than brute force.

Purity: Our purpose in life is to reveal God to everyone. We are told, "Be ye therefore perfect, even as your Father in heaven is perfect" (Matthew 5:48). Even though you may feel that you fall far short of this lofty goal, discipline yourself to keep eternally at it. Purity of soul, mind, heart, and body produce purity of motive, thought, feeling, expression, and action. This is a most important area that you can and must do something about.

Renunciation: It is very clear that there are certain things people simply cannot do if they are to enter into "the kingdom of Heaven" (the whole consciousness) and find "eternal life" (balanced, purposeful being). This means that you must

---

[5]Krishnamurti, *At the Feet of the Master* (Wheaton, IL: Theosophical Publishing House, 1984).

change your consciousness and give up doing whatever may impede your effectiveness as a person. Harmful mental, emotional, and physical habits and practices must all be subjected to renunciation. Divest yourself of anything and everything unlike the nature of God.

Discipline: How we admire someone who has control, who is kind, gentle, loving and understanding, who handles himself or herself well, and says all the right things. These character traits don't just happen; you "happen" them by building a consciousness of discipline. The mind loves to roam; it is a wanderer. But you have a will, and its purpose is to pattern itself upon God's will, which is the balanced harmony and wholeness of all perfect qualities.

In learning the soul lessons, which is the work of a lifetime, we develop certain desirable soul qualities. These include: beauty, compassion, tenderness, meekness, humility, patience, joy, harmony, honesty, integrity, goodness, restraint, and, eventually, a glimmer of truth. The attainment of these is the fruit of mastering the lessons of the soul.

THE MENTAL SELF

Some modern metaphysical spiritual teachings, including Religious Science, teach that God is Mind, and that we are mind. This, of course, is true, but there must be a full understanding of what it implies. As important as the mind is, there is more to our consciousness than the mental. The most accurate concept is that *Consciousness is the only Reality,* and that we are consciousness. Affirm: *I am consciousness. I am consciousness.* Let it sink in. Let it register in your subconscious consciousness.

Consciousness is the sum total of your thoughts, feelings, attitudes, beliefs, concepts, experiential conditioning, and your spiritual awareness, which formulate the causative faction of your identity, your experiences, and your state of being. You can readily see that consciousness is the only reality, and that your personal, individual consciousness is what you really are. Accepting this as the basic principle determining your personal destiny, and realizing that you can actually change your consciousness and rebuild it in optimum terms, is what this teaching is all about.

This is not a book about religion, philosophy, science, or psychology, per se, but rather a composite of all four in a practical metaphysical and mystical approach to building consciousness, thereby enhancing individual identity and increasing personal effectiveness. The first two chapters gave a comprehensive explanation of your mind and how to use it. Let us now consider its functions and use in building your consciousness, your character, and your identity as a spiritual being.

In the listing of the seven levels of your "self," your mind—or mental self—is in the middle, between the higher self and the lower self. In other words, the mind can go either way—up or down, spiritual or material, true or false, positive or negative. The mind has the faculty of choice and self-determination. Decision and selection are vitally important. They determine your dominion, power, authority, and identity. You are much more than a mental being, but the way you use your thinking, reasoning mind determines what kind of being you are.

Your mind is not your whole self—just part of it—but its use or misuse determines what you are. This is one of the most ancient of all teachings. As the Bible says, "Behold, I set before you this day a blessing and a curse; a blessing, if ye obey the commandments of the Lord your God . . . And a curse, if ye will not obey the commandments (Deuteronomy 11:26, 27, 28). Choose you this day whom ye will serve" (Joshua 24:15).

THE EMOTIONAL SELF

An important thing to remember while analyzing all of these different aspects of your self, is that each higher level has transcendence and dominion over all others below it. The universal has dominion over the six levels below. So, accordingly, your mind has dominion over your emotional or feeling nature. Many people believe just the opposite, and let the emotional self run rampant and out of control. This cannot be allowed to happen. Feelings, emotions, urges, drives, motivations, and desires are important in the structure of your complete self, but you must correct, control, and direct them. That is why your thoughts are so important, why they must be directed toward these three aspects of your self—the universal, the spiritual, and the soul.

Love, of course, is the greatest of all feelings and emotions, simply because it is more than feeling and emotion. It is of the spiritual nature more than of the human. That is why it is called the *summum bonum*—the supreme good—the greatest thing in the world. The Bible tells us that "love is the fulfilling of the law" (Romans 13:10).

If you have a self filled with love, everything will work out, but if you have everything else and do not have love, you are doomed to fail. (See I Corinthians 1:13). Love is of the universal, the spiritual and the soul, but it must be expressed on human levels by thought, feeling, and action. That is why the emotional level must be completely cleansed of anything and everything but love. It is done through the use of a technique called "Denials and Affirmations." It is a conscious process of replacing any and all negative feelings with positive loving ones, thereby reeducating your subconscious and building a loving consciousness. The Bible says, "Perfect love casteth out fear" (I John 4:18).

Your consciousness is your predominant inner nature—what you think and feel, what you are. It is the cause of all your experience: personally, physically, materially, and in the world of experience and relationships. You can readily see that how you feel about yourself, other people, and everything else in life, determines who and what you are.

THE PHYSICAL SELF

You have a body, but you are not your body. Most people, when they say "myself," refer primarily to their body, but we see that the self is much more: it is an integration of all seven levels. Your body is a magnificent part of you, but it is not all of you. Your body is spirit manifested in substance, form, and function, embodying the previous five levels: universal, spiritual, soul, mental, and emotional. They are all contained within your physical body. Is it any wonder that the Psalmist exclaims, "I will praise thee; for I am fearfully and wonderfully made" (Psalms 139:14)?

Your body is created as the external expression of your soul, so that it may function outwardly and gain this level of experience for its growth and unfoldment. The body does not act by itself; it is acted upon. It is subject to the commands of the personal will, which is activated by the individual mind; its structure and functions are greatly influenced by the personal consciousness (emotional, mental, soul, and spiritual).

The important thing to realize is that all the parts of yourself are interrelated. They interpenetrate each other, whereby each level of yourself is both cause and effect. It is necessary to recognize and maintain these relationships, and take care of each area of your being, so that you function as a whole being.

This book is about the proper care and use of all aspects of the self, with emphasis on consciousness. However, the importance of the body cannot be overlooked, because, as we have said, it is the outer manifestation of consciousness. In addition, of course, the genetic function of the individual and the race is performed through the body. All these factors are recognized when the body is called the temple of the Spirit.

In addition to maintaining an overall high and affirmative consciousness, and a joyous will to live, it is necessary to take care of the body with proper diet, rest, and exercise. Ample information and instruction in these areas are readily available. The bottom line is: learn about your body and take care of it; it is the only one you have. It is made to last until you leave the earth plane and graduate to a higher level of expression, which is, of course, the natural progression for everyone. But while you have a body, take care of it! Don't wait! The time is now. As one near-centenarian lamented, "If I had known I was going to live this long, I would have taken better care of myself!"

The Material Self

As you recognize all seven levels of the self, it is necessary to understand that everything is part of you, including everything that ever was, is now, or ever will be. The human being—your self—is a magnificent, eternal, infinite being that has lived forever.

As inspiring as this may be, your immediate concern is the present, the here and now, and the crucial importance of dealing properly with all the tangible things of human life. This includes possessions such as houses, appliances, and automobiles; great cities and highway systems; and all the natural wonders, from forests and rivers and mountains to deserts and swamps. Everything that has been created from the One Source, and everything built by human beings is in some way a part of your self.

Your environment is an important part of your experience. You cannot escape from it, nor should you want to, but you must not give it the power to control you. Obviously, your environment, natural and manufactured, affects you, but you are superior to it. You have the capacity to control it by transcending it. Remember, you are a universal, spiritual being, going through a human and material experience on the way toward complete and perfect unfoldment of your real self. You are embodied in your own creation and it is embodied in you, but you must maintain the identity of your true self in your consciousness. It is all a matter of perspective. Possessions cannot be allowed to possess you.

Maintain your consciousness of peace and freedom. You embody the five elements of earth, air, fire, water, and space. They are yours to use; they are your building blocks. Through the great tools given to you (the levels of the self), you have the capacity and ability to fully express your magnificent unlimited potential.

Keep your vision clear. Keep your options open. Do not let yourself be engulfed and distracted by trivia. You may own things—but do not let them own you. Follow the dictates of your higher self. You are the monarch of all that you survey. Act as though you own the earth, because you surely do! Claim your divine inheritance! Rise above places, possessions, and things. Establish personal dominion. Believe in yourself! You are human, but you are more than human. You are also God as human. You are in charge of yourself! Don't let this happen to you:

> But man, proud man,
> Drest in a little brief authority,
> Most ignorant of what he's most assur'd,
> His glassy essence, like an angry ape,
> Plays such fantastic tricks before high heaven
> As make the angels weep.[6]

---

[6] W. Shakespeare, *Measure for Measure,* Act II, scene 2, ll. 117–122.

Align yourself with your own magnificence. Make the most of yourself by identifying with the Higher Self. Relate the things of the world to the Great No Thing, and you will begin to be your self.

YOUR SELF-IMAGE

How do you see yourself? What picture of yourself do you impress upon the photographic plate of your subconscious? It is important that you see yourself not so much the way you are, but the way you want to be. If you get the picture of yourself at your highest and best, and hold your focus upon it, you will become the image and likeness of your self-image.

It is up to you to be diligent in seeing that your "self" (the small "me") becomes the enlargement of your "Self" (the large "Me"). Neither external appearances and circumstances, nor the concepts and impressions of others, have anything to do with it. Jesus admonished us, "Judge not according to the appearance, but judge righteous judgment" (John 7:24). In other words, look deep within yourself and see what is really there. "If therefore thine eye be single, thy whole body shall be full of light" (Matthew 6:22).

You are a bright, beautiful, wonderful, perfect child of God. See yourself that way. The beauty of the infinite is your beauty now. You have marvelous inner gifts of consciousness that will help you see yourself the way you really are: vision, insight, visualization, and imagination. Be persistent in seeing what you want to see, and that true picture—that reality—will come through bright and clear.

Identity

> I am here, but I am not here.
> I have a body, but I don't live in my body.
> I have a mind, but my life transcends it.
> I have a heart, but my life pulsates with a
> stronger beat.

I have a soul, but my life does not end there.
All of these — body, mind, heart, soul —
    Live in me, not I in them.
These are my servants — my tools
With which I build my life.

My life is God's Life
Living itself through me.
"I love, yet not I,
It is Christ that liveth my life."[7]

CORRECTING SELF-IMAGE

In acting, and indeed in all walks of life, you can only be balanced and successful if you work on your self-concept and self-image, building your consciousness of yourself as an aware, adjusted, confident, effective human being. Two steps are necessary: 1) The false ego must be dissolved; 2) the true ego must be affirmed.

This is usually just called *ego,* a word that was once respectable. It was spelled with a capital *E* and meant the Self — what you really are — your spiritual individuality. With the advent of Freudian psychology, *ego,* with a small *e,* was used to designate the outer, human, lesser self; while *Ego,* with a capital *E,* was used to refer to the higher self, just as it had originally. Therefore, some confusion exists in the use of the word. When *ego* is used, it usually refers to an intensely selfish, self-centered person — an egomaniac, an egocentric. An egotistical person is said to have an "ego problem" and is usually looked down upon and avoided by others.

A healthy personal ego is based upon the true Ego and indicates balanced, pleasant, joyous, capable individuals who know who they are and where they are going. They will be careful not to let personality get in the way of individuality, which is what they really are. The false ego puts an exagger-

---

[7] Previously unpublished poem, written by Donald Curtis.

ated emphasis upon the personality, which comes from the Greek word, *persona,* meaning *mask.*

Your personality—the false ego—masks what you really are. If you think only of your personality traits and outer appearance you are focused on the wrong things. Your accomplishments actually come more from what you *are* than from what you say, do, or look like.

False ego holds you back from the expression of your individuality, and eventually from your true potential. Handling the false ego may well be the real work of your lifetime. I know it has been mine. I have told you about some of the challenges that my false ego caused early in my life, but they didn't stop there. My false ego did help me to some extent, but then it held me back until I learned something about how to contact and express the true Ego—individuality—instead of personality. I'll tell you more about that a little later on.

When I first was presented with big time acting career opportunities in Hollywood, my false ego and personality stood in my way. I had talent and ability, but I was thinking too much about myself. When I was cast opposite a famous motion picture star, I would start to worry about how I looked or sounded. When I was overly concerned about whether I could carry it off, or whether I was just a farmer's kid not ready for the opportunities which had come my way, I would get scared.

One day when I was needed for a scene in a picture I was doing, I was late getting in front of the camera. I had been in my dressing room, fussing with my makeup. The director was furious. "Get in the scene," he thundered, "and forget your damned face!"

It was some of the best direction I ever received. What he was really saying was, "Forget your little self and be your real self." New concepts are continually introduced to help humanity move to a higher vibration. At the level of our false ego, this presents an interesting challenge.

The true Ego is a matter of being centered in the higher self instead of in the lower self, in the individuality rather than just the personality. When I became a minister, I had to learn this principle all over again, the hard way, from the very beginning.

It is my hope that by sharing some of my experiences, you will be motivated to apply some of these principles and techniques to your own life as you keep moving on the upward path, in whatever line of endeavor you are engaged. There are no shortcuts. None of the lessons can be avoided or evaded. All roads lead up the mountain, and we all make it to the summit, one step at a time. The important things are to know who you are and where you are going, to have a purpose in life, to set your goals, to believe in yourself, to keep your own counsel, to pay attention to your self-concept and self-image, to help others, and to have a grand time living.

When you do these things you will be making heaven happen right here and now. You won't have to worry about whether or not you are going to heaven or hell some day. If you are right within yourself, you will be in heaven already; if not, it is obvious where you are! What happens to you beyond your human experience will be an extension of what you are here. There are no such places as a literal heaven or a literal hell; they are states of consciousness. Everything comes from within yourself, here and hereafter.

Religious Beliefs

One way to build a foundation for consciousness is to take a look at your actual religious beliefs. Everyone has a tie to some "religious" system, and it can be used as a base while giving you the freedom to find God within yourself. If your traditional or formal religious affiliation is helping you, then you are on the right track. If not, then you should give some consideration to what we are discussing right now.

I have found inspiration in all religious and spiritual approaches. It is not necessary for you to join any church, denomination, or group, but it is essential for you to establish your relationship with God within yourself. I was brought up a Methodist, became an agnostic (or a "neglectnic"), sought solace in Catholicism, attended various Protestant denominations, worshiped in synagogues and mosques, and sat at the feet of gurus in the Himalayas; I have been instructed by masters in India, and meditated with Zen monks in Japan. They are all one. God is constantly revealing Himself in everything. It is up to you to recognize Him. Nature is the great teacher in our life. No matter what path you take, you will never find anything beyond what nature reveals.

"I must go to India. I must go to India!" I exclaimed to my friend and teacher, Manly Palmer Hall, near the beginning of my intense spiritual quest.

"Why do you need to go to India?"

"To find God," I replied.

"Listen," the wise philosopher counseled, "If you can't find God in Brooklyn, you are not going to find Him in India."

I listened, and followed Mr. Hall's direction. I did go to India, but not until much later, and when I did go there and many other places throughout the world on my spiritual quest, I took with me what I had already found within myself—the immanence and personalness of God. I do not believe it is possible to live a balanced life without this inner spiritual sense. At any rate, it is necessary to me. Everything contributes to it, even problems and difficulties.

I do not want to analyze or criticize any religious denomination or group that is spiritually oriented to helping its adherents find God. Unfortunately, this is not always the case. "Churchianity" often takes the place of Christianity, and rigid fundamentalist denominationalism often chokes out the purpose of religion, which is to unite the worshiper with God.

Ask yourself, "Is the religious approach I am following bringing me closer to God?" If it is, go all the way with it—until it is time for you to move ahead to the next phase of your quest. All extant religious groups exist for a purpose; otherwise they would die out, as so many have in the past. Therefore, if some denomination, group, or approach continues to function, there must be a reason for it, and it must continue to help people, even though this help may be only to reveal what is wrong to believe and do!

Develop your awareness and spiritual perceptiveness so that you detect these things for yourself. You don't have to go backward, or stay in a sterile relationship. Go forward. Find God within yourself. Seek understanding, awareness, inspiration, wisdom, and enlightenment within yourself through the regular practice of meditation, along with your outer, objective studies. Avail yourself of the great experiences that are available to you from within yourself. The New Thought and true New Age churches, groups, and teachers will help you find the way. Believe in yourself, and know that your true self will show you the way.

Personal Realization

I believe in myself. I know that the life work of my personal, human self is to find my True Self. I know that there is One Presence and One Power in the Universe, God the Good Omnipotent, present and active in my life and in all of my affairs. God is all of me. I am that part of God which I can understand.

I am attuned to my Universal Self today. I am a child of the Universe. I exist beyond time or space. I have always been and I will always be. I live forever, one day at a time. I express my Universal Self fully in all that I am and do. I am a spiritual being going through a human experience on the way toward complete and perfect expression of my Real Self.

God is individualized in me. The Divine Light is individualized in me as the Christ of my being. I am an expression of my Spiritual Self at all times. I am a living soul. My Soul Self expresses my Universal Self and my Spiritual Self. My soul is the embodiment of Spirit and Light. My soul is filled with

God. My soul is filled with the Infinite. My soul grows and expands as I assist God in building more stately mansions in my soul.

My Mental Self is an active entity within the Supreme Being. I think, I reason, I select, I choose, I initiate action. I am constantly learning. I gain in knowledge. I develop wisdom and I attain understanding. I give thanks for the magnificent scope of my Mental Self.

As my Emotional Self, I am a creature of feeling. I am filled with love. I sing with exultation as I feel the free, full flow of Life surging through me, integrating me and making me whole. My Emotional Self feels gratitude for the wonder and beauty of Life.

My Physical Self is the outer manifestation of my Inner Self. My body is Spirit in form. I am a tangible outer expression, in form and function, of the infinite, invisible, subjective factors of my consciousness. My Physical Self is an instrument and tool of my mind and soul. I experience vital health in my body as all levels of my being are attuned in integrated wholeness.

My Material Self is comprised of objects, things, and possessions, which are a projection of my consciousness, and which I use in my everyday life. I possess things, but I do not let them possess me. Divine order and correct action prevail in every aspect of my Material Self. I give thanks for this aspect of my Self.

All levels of my Self are perfectly aligned and attuned, and my Self is whole. Thank You, Father-Mother God. And so it is.

CHAPTER 4

YOU CAN DO IT!

Many people are unhappy with their work and are spending a major part of their lives doing things they don't want to do or don't like to do. This causes tension, resistance, pressure, and stress, resulting in a number of psychosomatic physical conditions and illnesses. Frustration and resistance in consciousness produce confusion and stress in the mind and in the emotional nature, which in turn project into the body, causing both organic and functional disorders.

You can easily prove this by observing yourself. Start by assuming that any condition, problem, or malfunction of your body is the result of negative mental and emotional states within yourself. You will find that you can easily relate any physical problems to what you have been feeling and thinking about. Since most of these situations are work-related, it is important to find happiness, harmony, and joy in your work. Someone once said, "Find out what you enjoy doing and you will never have to work another day in your life."

You must enjoy whatever endeavor you embark upon, or you will not really want to do it: if you do not want to do it, you will not do it well, if you really want to do it, you will find a way to do it, and enjoy it, and succeed at it. Desire and confidence are of twin importance. You are unique. There is something you can do that no one else can do. And something you can do better than anything else you do.

FIVE STEPS TO SUCCESS

Successful accomplishment is rarely easy, even for those possessing desire and confidence. Many an "overnight success" has worked long and hard for the rewards gained. But we can all succeed if we follow simple plans or strategies to help us along our path. Over the years I have developed these five important steps:

1) Decide what you want to do.

2) Learn all you can about it.

3) Develop the necessary consciousness.

4) Do whatever is necessary to do it.

5) Keep eternally at it.

Deciding: In business there is an axiom that says, "Those who do not make up their own minds will follow those who do."

What do you want to do? It is up to you to decide. You can do whatever you want to do. You can be whatever you want to be. Believe this. Know it! Do not depend upon anyone else, nor allow anyone else to tell you how to spend your life or what you can or cannot do. It is your province, and yours alone. You are already halfway there when you make your decision.

Of course the choice of what you want to do cannot and should not be made casually nor quickly, nor should it be taken lightly. You are playing hardball for keeps when you make choices about your life. Do not make just any choice, either, simply because you think you should, or because others are pressing you for a decision.

Some people are late bloomers, while others are born with a knowledge of what they have come into this world to do. It is hard to imagine, for instance, that there was any doubt in Mozart's mind as to what he was to be. He composed a symphony at the age of five, and went on to compose great music throughout his brief life.

If you need some input as to what you want to do, you might use the method that one father used in helping his five sons decide what occupation they were to follow. He asked each one in turn, "What do you want to do for people?"

"I want to teach people," answered the eldest son.

"Then you want to be a teacher."

"I want to feed people," said the next son.

"You want to be a restaurateur."

"I want to heal people," the third son answered.

"Then you want to be a doctor."

"I want to help people find God," said the fourth son.

"You want to be a minister."

When the time came for the youngest son to make his decision, the father asked him the same question he had asked his older brothers over the years: "What do you want to do for people?"

"I want to make people laugh," the young man stated.

"Then, obviously, you want to be a comedian."

"Yes, I know, Daddy. I have already decided."

He had — and he did. This story was told to me by one of Hollywood's leading comedians of an earlier day — who numbered a college president, a successful restaurant owner, an eminent physician, and a minister among his older brothers. The father had not told his sons what to do; he just helped them decide what they *wanted* to do.

Do not be concerned if you can't quite pinpoint what you want to do. Do not be reluctant because you are afraid you might make the wrong choice. Impossible: There are no wrong choices. As a guru once counseled me, "God may not tell you the right choice, but He will not let you make the wrong one."

Think about that, and affirm to yourself: *There is that which I have come into this world to do. I am guided and directed in finding what it is, and once it is revealed to me and I have decided to do it, I am strengthened and assisted by the One Power in doing it.*

This is a form of prayer for divine guidance. Prayer is talking to God—and then listening. Do not ask God what you are to do, but know that when you become still, He will tell you what your next step is. Make regular prayer a part of your life.

You may pursue several courses of action while you are finding what you really want to do. When I was quite young, I had a burning desire to be a writer, but somewhat later a different talent revealed itself and I studied and trained to be an actor. That was put on hold for a few years while I pursued a career as a college professor, and then, eventually, my desire to be an actor reasserted itself and my acting career unfolded.

The early years in Hollywood were exciting, but also filled with anxiety and frustration. The anxiety came from lack of real confidence in myself. Feelings of uncertainty and inferiority would come up at most inopportune times: when I was being interviewed for a leading role, or when I was before the cameras in an important scene, perhaps playing opposite a glamorous motion picture star. Suddenly I would feel that I was just a farm boy trying to get by with something I had no business trying to do. My uncertainty, of course, was picked up by the sensitive motion picture cameras, and several times I was replaced in important roles when the producers lost confidence in me because I had none in myself.

However, my desire to be a motion picture star was strong, and there had never been any place in my life for failure, so I hung in there, and as I gained confidence in myself, I started to get good roles again.

At this point, I had to learn to deal with other destructive feelings: frustration, envy, animosity, and pessimism. I was frustrated and disappointed because my career was not progressing as rapidly as I thought it should. I was not getting the leading roles I thought I deserved, and I reacted unpleasantly, with complaints and pessimism. I was envious and jealous of fellow actors who were getting the breaks, and I felt rejected and dejected. I did not yet understand how important positive attitudes are. It was much later that I came to realize that your thoughts can change your life.

During this period in my Hollywood career, disappointments accumulated until I became sardonic and cynical. People, including casting directors, avoided me—until I had an opportunity to try out for the part of a heavy in a John Wayne western. I got the part because my inner feelings of unhappiness and cynicism were picked up by the camera, showing a personality which was just right for a western bad guy. One heavy led to another, and I became typecast in a series of such roles. Adding acting ability to my cynical thoughts and feelings, I soon was in demand to play villains in a number of pictures.

But that wasn't what I wanted to do! I wanted to play leading, romantic roles. I wanted to be a star! Falling short of my goals intensified the dark side of my character, which in turn made me an even better bad guy. I accepted the roles because I needed to make a living for myself and my family, but I often asked myself, "What am I doing playing parts like these? I should be doing something more important! Why, I have been a college professor. And I could write better stuff than this!"

I continued playing heavies in innumerable pictures, but I sought other avenues of expression. I started teaching acting in a drama school, just as I had done when I was a graduate student at Northwestern University Theater Department, and when I was head of the Theater Department at Duquesne University. This changed my life. I discovered that I really liked teaching—not as much as acting, but it made me feel that I was doing something important, so I continued to both act and teach.

Then something wonderful happened to me! Metro-Goldwyn Mayer put me under contract to play parts in "A" pictures, with the promise of being developed into a leading player, which, in turn, could lead to becoming a Hollywood star.

This "break" was an example of how our thoughts change our life, although I was not aware of how the principle worked at the time. But here is what had happened: when my creative energies were turned toward teaching, my consciousness changed, and it showed in my personality and in my face. My anger, disappointment, envy, and negativity dissolved; I became joyous, cheerful, and enthusiastic again, thus moving out of the unattractive villain parts into handsome leading-man roles. My thoughts were changing my life!

I was very happy being a part of the "big time" and working with glamorous Hollywood people. I didn't have time to do much teaching, but I didn't miss it, except when I didn't have anything to do between pictures. Production would end on one film, and there might be a considerable period of time before the next one was ready to start.

During these periods of enforced idleness, my old feelings of frustration and discouragement would return. Needing to be busy all the time, I made some starts at writing. Remember, the desire to write had been one of my childhood goals. However, it really didn't come to anything, because every time I would get organized and start to write, the studio would call, assigning me to a production, and I would become completely involved in acting again, sometimes for months at a time. But I really only wanted to act in the first place—or so I thought. I was not aware of how my inner consciousness was continuing to formulate the pattern of my life. My thoughts were changing my life, and I still didn't know it.

I was an actor. I was doing what I had set out to do, with a considerable measure of success. I was getting better roles, higher billing, and making more money, but I wasn't really getting anywhere. I wasn't happy. I had a strong inner feeling, even though I still wanted to be a movie star, that there was something else I was to do.

It was at this time that I first heard Dr. Ernest Holmes speak. Shortly thereafter I started studying the Science of Mind with a view to becoming a minister and continuing my acting at the same time. Shortly thereafter I was ordained. Finally I gave up acting altogether.

During the many years I have been a minister, I have often been asked, "Don't you miss acting?" My answer is always the same: "Not a bit! In what other job could you play Hamlet every day of your life?"

Do you see how my thoughts have changed my life? All of my earlier goals: to become a writer, to become an actor, to become a teacher, are now combined in what I really wanted to be all the time, without knowing it. I had to grow into it by a succession of achievement steps, without which I would not have been ready for my life's work. My training and success in teaching, speaking, and acting have been invaluable to me as a person and as a minister.

My earlier endeavors produced challenges which could only be met through spiritual understanding. When the scope of spiritual unfoldment was revealed to me, there was no doubt in my mind what I was supposed to do with my life. When the time came, I knew it immediately, and I never hesitated. I knew I could do it.

Although I had no doubts, there were others who were not so sure at the beginning. One actor with whom I had worked over the years, but had lost touch with, stood looking at my name in front of the church where I was minister. "Is that the same Donald Curtis who played heavies in western pictures?" he demanded.

"Yes, he's the same," one of my associates responded.

"Well, I'll be . . . !" he exploded, "If he can do it, *anybody* can do it!"

That is true. Whatever it is, you can do it—if you want to, and if you know that you can.

Learning: The second step is not intended to help you decide what you are going to do; it *follows* the decision. When you come to the second step, you have already decided. If the second step came first, you might be diverted from making your decision. It has been said that if everyone knew all that was entailed in being a parent, the race would die out. If I had known what it takes to be a minister when I made my decision to become one, I might not have had the courage to make it. Your decision is not based upon knowledge; it is based upon inspiration, dedication, and commitment.

However, once you have made your decision, it is necessary to know everything there is to know about what you are setting out to do, so that you will be a success at it. Great responsibility goes with what you do. You are not just doing it for yourself, you are doing it because it is something that needs to be done, something that you are assigned to do, and something that will help others.

"God, please tell me about the peanut," prayed the young George Washington Carver.

"You have a mind of your own," came the answer. "Go and find out."

Obeying the command, George Washington Carver went to work to find out everything he could about the peanut, discovering hundreds of uses for it, to an extent that determined the entire economic structure of the South—all because of one man who decided to help his people. His knowledge of the peanut enabled him to fulfill his purpose in life.

Knowledge and understanding come through a combination of study, experience, and intuitive perception. You have a much greater chance of succeeding if you know what you are doing. Immerse yourself completely in everything having to do with your endeavor. If you really want to do what you have set out to do, your motivation will be strong and steady.

Once I became interested in metaphysics, religion, and all things spiritual, my appetite was insatiable. I took every class and seminar that came along, and read everything I could put my hands on. I studied incessantly, but it was not difficult because I really wanted to know. When your interest is aroused and you become inspired, something happens within yourself, which you cannot quell even if you want to. The more you learn about your subject, the more you want to know, and the more you know, the more you want to put into practice what you have learned.

When you start to *do* what you have been studying, you really start to learn. You are now playing for keeps. You will find out very quickly what you know and what you don't. There is a great deal to learn from on-the-job training. Experience is a great teacher. Trial and error and experimentation will teach you lessons you never knew existed. When you become a truly active, working part of what you have aspired to, knowledge, information, wisdom, understanding, and judgment will come to you through experience. They cannot be attained in any other way.

There is much that you can learn only by doing. It is a continuing process—the more you learn, the more effective and successful you become. When you stop learning, you stop growing. When you stop growing, you stop going anywhere.

When you first learned to drive a car, there were many things you needed to learn before you ever took the wheel. You studied about the car itself and learned the driving regulations. But once you sat in the driver's seat, the learning process really began. You "suited the action to the word, the word to the action."[1] What you previously only knew *about,* you started to *know.* What you had aspired to, you now became. The same process prevails in whatever you enter into, learn about, and start to do.

During my youthful days of dreaming about being an actor, I read about the theater voraciously, attended performances whenever I could, and acted in school plays continually. I learned about acting by combining study and experience. I wanted to devote my life to it, but the more I learned, the more I wanted to learn. It is an eternal axiom that the more you know the more there is to know. (Of course, I didn't know that then. I thought I knew all there was to know about it. Why, I had played the great roles in school and college productions; my training period was over. I was ready for Hollywood and Broadway!)

However, upon entering into those "sacred" precincts, I was rudely awakened. It wasn't exactly the way I had been taught! I was fired from my first Broadway role because I was too green, too inexperienced—I just didn't know how. I didn't know the things I later learned through experience.

Later, when I was inspired to be a minister and made the decision to become one, I really had no conception of what this entailed. Just as I had thought in Hollywood that one day I would wake up in the morning a movie star, without realizing the struggle, the blood, sweat, and tears that would be involved, when I dreamed of becoming a minister, I thought only of how wonderful it would be to stand before a large congregation and speak.

When I actually became a minister, I learned that, quite contrary to the popular conception that a minister only works one hour a week on Sunday, he is likely to be on the job seven days a week, twenty-four hours a day. However, the rewards are so great that no minister would have it any other way.

---

[1] W. Shakespeare, *Hamlet,* Act III, scene 2, l.19.

My observations about becoming an actor and a minister apply also to my continuing activity as a writer and a teacher. There are basic skills to be learned in any field, but essentially you learn about writing by writing, and you learn about teaching by teaching. (Unless the teacher learns at least as much as the student he is not much of a teacher.) Since my spiritual mission is largely one of teaching through speaking and writing, I am on a lifelong learning project. Try it in your chosen field. You'll like it.

After study and experience, the third major area of learning is intuitive spiritual inspiration and perception. The true teacher is your own higher self. If you want to know about something, ask it to tell you about itself, and it will do so.

You already know all there is to be known about everything. You may not know that you know it, but it is all stored in the Cosmic Data Bank to which your personal computer (your mind) has access. Learning through study and experience releases part of it, but the more productive process is the one of "tuning in"—unlocking the treasures of the universal subjective consciousness, which individualizes through you when you make contact with it and becomes a channel for its expression.

This is by far the highest and most productive method of learning. Explore it. Develop your sensitivity awareness. Follow the guidance of inspiration and motivation, and learn to trust your intuition. Your inner self is a great teacher. Can you think of anything or anyone more important than a good teacher?

Learn to think, meditate, and contemplate. The instruction is most explicit: "Be still, and know that I am God" (Psalms 46:10). It is literally true. Your real self is an individualization of God. God is all of you; you are that part of God which you can understand.

Wisdom and understanding are developed through the process of inner knowing. Solomon extols the virtues of wisdom:

> For wisdom is better than rubies; and all the things
> that may be desired are not to be compared to it.
> . . . Counsel is mine, and sound wisdom: I am un-
> derstanding; I have strength (Proverbs 8:11, 14).

Development of inner knowing is an essential part of the learning process. *Man* means *knower*. Be a knower!

Deciding to *do* and learning *about* are important steps as you move toward accomplishing your objective. But there is still more. You can make great decisions and learn all about everything, but unless you prepare yourself to follow through, it will come to nothing.

Preparing: We come now to an intangible building block in your structure of accomplishment, which may well be the most important of all. It is the realm of consciousness, which we have defined as the sum total of your thoughts, feelings, attitudes, experience, and spiritual awareness. Consciousness is what you are—your character, your essence, your quality. Consciousness has more to do with your attainment than any-thing else.

You have been developing your consciousness as you have made your decision and have been learning through study, experience, and intuition. By now you have literally be-come inwardly what you aspire to be outwardly. The only re-maining step is to actually do what you want to do, including everything that goes with it. We will find that the final, fourth step, when we come to it, is virtually automatic, because what you become in consciousness must manifest in form and actual experience.

How do you build consciousness? By being true to your ideal, and by keeping eternally at it. Decision, discipline, ded-ication, devotion, and determination are essential, but there is still something more. In motion pictures it is called "star quality." It is also called magnetism, and charisma. It is virtually indefinable, but it is necessary to have it if you are to attain the heights. It is of the soul, and it develops as you go along, when you are dedicated to ideal and purpose. It is your light and it shines through you. Others see it and are inspired by it. You do not need to do anything about it specifically. Just live by high, idealistic, spiritual principles, do your best, and be your best at all times. You become what you aspire to: think it, feel it, speak it, express it, and embody it.

What you are is more important than what you do. Fall in love with life and live it fully. Let the harmony and blessing of love shine from you to surround everyone and everything. Embody love in all that you are and do. Give thanks constantly. "Pray without ceasing" (I Thessalonians 5:17). Develop your inner spiritual being with affirmation, prayer, and meditation. Dwell in the realization that you are a perfect child of God, and that your life is the expression of this perfection. Build the consciousness and conviction that God's life is your life now.

Doing It: Through decision, investigation, and conviction, we come now to the fourth step: action. Action follows consciousness of conviction. You know that you have the abilities and the faith to do whatever you set out to do, but your life potential will not grow and multiply until you invest them in accomplishment. Conviction must be followed by action, or nothing happens. Remember, "If it is to be, it's up to me." You have come all this way. Now all you have to do is do it!

You have embarked upon the journey of your life. Everything you do is related to the fulfillment of what you have set out to do. No effort, no expense, no sacrifice is too great. Make up your mind to follow through on every detail. It may involve many tasks, some arduous and difficult, but you won't mind them, because you know where you are going, and how to get there.

Guarantee

I did my job today,
I gave all I had to give,
I was prepared for what I came to do,
I did the very best I could.

I know I could have done it better,
And that there are others who could reach a
    higher mark,
But I'm not ashamed of what I did today
Because I did the very best I could.

I have done much better many times before,
And tomorrow may do better than I've ever done,
But today I rest my case on what I did today,
Because I did the very best I could.

I plan to keep doing my best, to keep improving,
You'll always find me there at the appointed time,
Ready to do what God has given me to do,
And when it's done, you can be sure
That I did the very best I could.[2]

The widowed, black, mother held down two full-time jobs over many years in order to bring up her family of five children and send them to college. Finally, her youngest child—a son—finished college and was accepted for medical school.

"Mama, I'm not going to go," he stated.

"Son, you are going to medical school, and that's final! Why do you think I've been working so hard all these years? For you to quit now?"

"That's just it, Mama. I can't have you working so hard any longer!"

---

[2]D. Curtis, *Cosmic Awareness* (Dallas, TX: Christway Publications, 1984), p. 68.

"That's my business, Son. You leave that up to me. Your business is to go to medical school."

"But you're wearing yourself out, Mama!"

"Pshaw! I'm not wearing myself out. Why, Son, I don't even get tired. You see, I've got a glory! My son is going to medical school. I've got a glory!"

There you have it. Your "glory" will give you the joy, the energy, and the resolve to do whatever it is you need to do.

Albert Schweitzer had a "glory." From the time of his childhood, he felt a deep need to serve his fellow man. He decided to work until he was 30 years old in the fields of music, philosophy, and theology, and then devote the rest of his life to service. Ignoring the many who tried to discourage him, he entered medical school and obtained a medical degree. He then bought medicines and hospital supplies, and went with his wife to Central Africa, where he built a mission hospital and ministered to the African people for many years.

Dr. Schweitzer was renowned throughout the world for his dedication and his contributions to humanity. He knew what he wanted to do, and he did whatever was necessary to do it. He was true to his "glory."

What do you need to do to follow your star? Change jobs? Move to a new locale? Alter your life style? Go back to school? Write a book? Sell your business and your house, and homestead in Alaska? Learn a trade? Take flying lessons? Paint pictures? Act in the community theatre, sing in the church choir? Take dancing lessons? Get active in community affairs? Run for public office?

I am not suggesting that you must change. But if you are not happy with what you are doing, if you are not following your "glory," then do whatever you need to, to accomplish what you want. Thousands of men and women just like you and me are coming to this realization every day, and are doing something about it. What are you doing about it?

Take your life in hand. Develop the resolve of the one who said, "The difficult we do immediately. The impossible takes a little longer." In a speech, Robert Muller once said that the problem with the world today is that not enough people are attempting the impossible. Don't let this be said of you. Gather your forces, go forward, and tenaciously pursue your goal.

Keeping At It: Your pathway toward achievement may not always be easy. It probably won't be. Someone has said that just because you decide to do some good in the world, it doesn't mean that people are going to stand in line to help. They are more likely to throw rocks in your path. It seems that way sometimes, but you really have no choice but to keep on keeping on.

Keep A-Goin'!

Ef you strike a thorn or rose,
    Keep a-goin'!
Ef it hails, or ef it snows,
    Keep a-goin'!
'Taint no use to sit an' whine,
When the fish ain't on yer line;
Bait yer hook an' keep a-tryin'—
    Keep a-goin'![3]

There are many instances of men and women who refused to accept defeat, remembering this assurance: "If you have faith, as a grain of mustard seed, ye shall say to this mountain, Remove hence to yonder place; and it shall remove; and nothing shall be impossible unto you" (Matthew 17:20).

Nothing shall be impossible unto you if you have the will to succeed! "Whatever your mind can conceive and believe, you can achieve." Your attitude must always be upbeat and

[3]F. L. Stanton, "Keep A-Goin" in *One Hundred and One Famous Poems,* ed. Roy J. Cook (Chicago, IL: The Reilly and Lee Publishers, 1958), p. 135.

expectant. Never, never, never give up. Never abandon your dream.

The way you handle difficulties is one of the keys to achievement. You cannot let difficulties discourage you; they are blessings in disguise. Meet each one of them by saying, *Thank You, Father-Mother God, for this evidence of your love for me. Through this means do I grow.* In this way you turn difficulties into opportunities. Do not identify a difficulty as a problem. Don't even use the word! Think of a problem as a challenge, and it will no longer be a block or a threat to you. The progression goes like this: difficulty, problem, challenge, opportunity, privilege, and blessing.

When you consider it a privilege to triumph over difficulties, solve problems, and meet challenges, everything you undertake is an opportunity to grow. That's what we are here in this life for anyway, isn't it—to live, to love, to learn, to laugh, and to grow? Remember, it is not you who is doing the job, anyway. As Jesus said, ". . . the Father that dwelleth in me, he doeth the works" (John 14:10). You are a channel through which mighty creative forces flow. Know it, and you will do your job and fulfill your purpose.

No matter how difficult it is, or how long it takes to reach your ultimate goal of fulfillment, you are a winner every step of the way. What is the hurry? Why the worry? What would you like to be doing instead of what you are doing? Apply yourself to the business at hand. Don't waste your life in pursuits that you are not interested in. Get your guidance and your motivation from within, and then express yourself fully through your work.

You do not work to make a living; you work to express yourself. Work is the great healer. Give thanks for work. Exult in it! Set up impossible tasks and go forth to conquer them. You never know what you can do until you try. Enjoy what you are doing, every moment.

The old farmer constantly complained about how much work he had to do and how difficult it was. He longed for the time when he would no longer need to work. "There's going to come a time when I'm not going to work another day in my life," he constantly affirmed.

Finally, he finished his earthly sojourn and moved on to the next level of his eternal existence. It was wonderful! There were servants to do every task and to fulfill his slightest wish. He had absolutely nothing to do but luxuriate in eternal bliss. He had never been happier.

However, the day came when his idyllic existence began to pall. He became restive and irritable, and finally called for the head attendant. "Bring me some work to do!" he commanded.

"I'm sorry, sir. That's one thing we cannot do. We cannot give you any work to do."

"Why not? I thought I could have anything I want in heaven."

"That's true, sir, but where you are there is no work to do. That's the hell of it."

Fortunately, as a self-achiever you will never have that experience. Express yourself fully through work each day. Balance your life with rest and recreation, of course, but never be afraid of work. "Plan your work, and work your plan." It is impossible to do enough work to make you tired. Fatigue and exhaustion do not come from work; they come from tension, pressure, fear, stress, resistance, and anxiety. Your work reinforces you. You are supposed to work, and you have the privilege of going about it on your own terms. Avoid excuses and procrastination, which only put a burden upon you. It isn't what you do that makes you tired; it is what you don't do. What you don't do can make you ill.

For instance, I have a tremendous energy dynamic that awaits my direction for constructive work. However, I sometimes fritter away my time and energy with details and the writing part of my job gets delayed.

After I had finished writing one of my books (I write my books in longhand — I can establish and maintain the flow from my subconscious better that way), I delayed starting a new one that was nudging at me. The pressure started to build up, but I ignored it. Before long, I experienced a severe pain in my right arm, and I could find nothing to relieve it. I was really suffering.

I told my young son about it, and he observed, "You haven't been writing lately, Daddy. Maybe your pain is God telling you to get busy on the book." I started to write there and then, and I have never stopped. And I haven't had that particular pain again.

What is causing you pain? What is God telling you to do? What are you waiting for? Whatever it is you are meant to do, you can do it! You are a genius at being you. All you need to do to find complete fulfillment is to express yourself fully — now.

PERSONAL REALIZATION

The free, full flow of life is surging through me, moving me into full and perfect expression of my Real Self. I am determined to make the most of myself in every way. I commit myself to doing that work which expresses me and benefits others. A mighty dynamic of energy and power flows through me, motivating me to do that which God has given me to do. I go with the flow.

My decision is to devote myself to doing that which God has given me to do. I know I can do it. I tune in for inner guidance, and then I go to work. God does the work through me. He is the Source. I am the channel. We are a perfect team. God is the Boss. I am the servant. I do whatever He tells me to do. I am firm in my decision.

I am a learner. I know that knowledge is power. I investigate, I study, I experiment. I learn. I am a master in my field of endeavor. I am organized. I am persistent, dedicated, and committed. I know who I am, what I am doing, where I am going, and how to get there. I move steadily toward my goal.

I learn from experience. Every challenge lifts me to greater heights of improvement and achievement. I never stand still. I am about my Father's business at all times. I have a glory. I revel in the experience of it.

I am positive and constructive in thought, feeling, and action. My consciousness is high. I am a winner. I press on to victory. I live both on the inner and the outer. My strength comes from within. I use my strength wisely and well.

I release all concern about anything and everything. "The Lord is my light and my salvation; whom shall I fear? the Lord is the strength of my life; of whom shall I be afraid?" (Psalms 27:1).

I am filled with strong and steadfast faith. Nothing can disturb me. Nothing can deter me. I have complete confidence in myself and my abilities. My inner conviction strengthens me. I have complete faith in the One Presence and the One Power which is God.

Thank You, Father-Mother God, for Life, and the privilege of living it. Thank You for Truth, and the privilege of knowing it. Thank You for work, and the privilege of doing it. And so it is.

CHAPTER 5

KNOW WHERE YOU ARE GOING

The following dialogue could well describe the situation in which many people find themselves.

"How is everything going?"

"Well, I've got bad news and I've got good news. I'll give you the bad news first: we're lost."

"We're *lost?* And what's the good news?"

"We're making very good time!"

They simply do not know where they are going. Instead of formulating a plan and following it, they run around in circles, gaining speed and momentum but going nowhere. Are you one of these rudderless ships? If so, let me share an effective life research technique called the Golden Bridge, which has appeared in some of my other books. It may help you discover where you are going.

THE GOLDEN BRIDGE

The Golden Bridge is the actual completion of inner identification with the creative process. As you build the Golden Bridge, you are constructing a path upon which to travel to completion and accomplishment. By this process you form an invisible structure upon which to build your life. It defines where you are going, and provides a means for getting there.

The Golden Bridge utilizes all your creative faculties. It takes chance and effort out of your activities; it dissolves the barriers of time and space by building within you an awareness of purpose and completion. The use of the Golden Bridge enables you to transcend human failings and weaknesses, and lifts you into a consciousness of your true place in the great scheme of things. Let's learn how to use it now.

Become completely relaxed; detach your mind from all concerns and random thoughts. Remove all personal effort as you become still and identify yourself with the indwelling reality. Visualize light and inner peace and beauty, and let a feeling of power and strength generate within you. Let yourself become filled with spiritual fuel that provides the thrust to project you into new and vital experience. Picture yourself as a magnificent and powerful rocket being projected along a beautifully arching trajectory into new spheres of understanding and experience. What you are doing in inner visualization looks something like figure 2.

Jesus said, "I go to prepare a place for you" (John 14:2). The "I" is your inner creative awareness. Visualization, imagination, and realization are its natural capacities. You are this "I." Send it ahead and let it prepare the place for you. Trust it completely. It is intuition inspired by spiritual realization. It is your real self. Through it you build the Golden Bridge of your life.

Where you are   Where you are going

Figure 2. The Golden Bridge.

This technique may be applied to any area of your experience, no matter how small it may be—from a single moment to eternity. The Golden Bridge enables you to know where you are going. Once you have spanned it in inner consciousness, you can then return and travel it in the action of experience, without any peril of losing your way.

Technique: When your inner consciousness reaches your destination—even though the outer self may still need to go through plans, problems, and worldly actions—the inner self has already reached its destination and achieved its goal. It is simply a matter of reaching absolute conviction. There is no better way to convince yourself that you can do a thing than to actually do it. When you travel the Golden Bridge, you arrive at your destination *first,* as preparation for starting on your way.

Suppose you were to take a trip to a distant country where you have never been. You would arrange the trip with your travel agent, who would help you make plans and tell you what you could expect; you would study travel folders, and learn about the language and customs of the place you were to visit. You would provide yourself with tickets and all the necessary items to take on the trip. You would prepare yourself completely for a pleasant journey. In essence, you would take the trip many times, vicariously, before you actually started on the physical journey. You would be there in consciousness long before you ever left home.

So it is with the Golden Bridge. But it is more than just an imaginary journey. It is complete preparation for what is to follow. We both misunderstand and underestimate the true function and power of the imagination. You are what and where you are because you have first imagined it, consciously or subconsciously.

The Golden Bridge speeds up the process, making it easier. The Golden Bridge is the *direct* path. It avoids detours, twistings and turnings, pain and suffering, misdirections and discouragements. With the Golden Bridge, you do not lose your way.

Visualize the Golden Bridge arching straight up to the summit of a high mountain, bypassing the winding, twisting road beneath. The mountain, of course, represents achievement and enlightenment attained through growth and experience. It represents the distance you travel as you keep moving upward.

The narrow, rocky road represents the long, slow, perilous trek, often fraught with false starts, frequent detours, dead ends, toil, and suffering. Eventually it too reaches the summit. But the Golden Bridge provides a straight path to the top, enabling you to progress more surely and more rapidly by developing your full inner resources. It may take us many lifetimes to reach the summit, but remember, we all make it eventually!

The visual representation of the Golden Bridge should be firmly fixed in your mind as a master symbol for meditation and inner spiritual work. Even though you may sometimes get confused in dealing with life's problems, you can always get back on the right track by visualizing this straight path. You can never get lost when you stay on the Golden Bridge.

The Golden Bridge is a means of cooperating with the creative law of life. It enables you to use the power within you for the real business of life—growth and accomplishment on every level. It is one means of making your personal will one with divine will. Constant inner work will enable you to discover that will and cooperate with it.

The Golden Bridge technique may be used to prepare the way for any segment of activity or experience—an hour, a day, a week, a month, a year, a lifetime. Start by using it to span one day. Mentally cut through any doubts and anticipated difficulties until the path of the day is projected straight and true before you. In this way you arrive mentally at your destination before you actually start the trip.

You have no idea of the freedom and ease with which you will travel. You will gain direction and certainty that will enable you to meet every situation with confidence and power. Once you *know* everything is going to be all right — the conviction you build with your Golden Bridge — you will not be concerned with minor difficulties that may arise. The very fact that you have built your conviction in itself projects an authority and power that keeps difficulties from arising and causes everything to work out properly.

Construct your Golden Bridge for each day as soon as possible upon awakening. Get perfectly still, and travel step by step to the end of the day, progressively building the conviction that you are actually there, doing the things you are visualizing and stating, and that they are complete. Make your statements aloud if possible, for it will keep your mind on a straight track and build a stronger inner feeling.

Continue until you have covered your entire day. Give special attention to important appointments, decisions, and projects. Take the affirmative approach, and keep at it until the picture is clear and your conviction is strong. Cover everything, no matter how large or how small. The results you achieve depend upon the thoroughness of your inner mental work. Refuse to let your mind dwell upon anything other than what you want it to accept.

Once you form the habit of building the Golden Bridge, you will never try to do anything without it. The longer you work with this technique, the more proficient you will become, and the easier it will be to do. As you do your inner job well, you will be able to handle anything that comes up.

There may be times during the day when you will need to become quiet and do some repair work on your Golden Bridge. Or, you may need to alter the original design. Don't let this upset you; just do it. Flow with life; be flexible and adaptable, but always work from a solid inner structure.

Having completed your Golden Bridge, release it — forget about it, and go on with what you have to do. The structure is there and will automatically provide the pattern for the action that follows. You will be amazed by the results you achieve, and how much more enjoyable life becomes.

Retrospection: Retracing your steps is a technique that goes hand in hand with the Golden Bridge. Let's suppose you have traveled your Golden Bridge — successfully or unsuccessfully — throughout the day. You are now back in bed, where you awoke to start your day many hours before. No matter what the day has been like, get quiet inside and deliberately go back over the Golden Bridge of your day in reverse order. Start from where you are, and retrace your steps through the evening, dinner, the afternoon, lunch, the morning, and all the way back to when you awoke. Fix everything so that it is right.

If a situation was handled badly, correct it in your mind, and rehearse it visually, with thought, word, action, and feeling, until it is right. Forgive yourself and others. If you were wrong, admit it. Erase all unpleasant memories, impressions, and confusion, and replace them with the corrected ones. Your subconscious mind will retain what you instruct it to retain. Correct your mistakes and fix things that went wrong, giving particular attention to your thoughts and attitudes and what you said and felt. This is exactly what a director does after a rehearsal of a performance that needs improvement.

You will cleanse your mind, your memory, and your emotional state of everything other than what you want to have remain there as a permanent and constructive part of your consciousness. You will balance the mental, emotional, and spiritual budget. You will sleep better than you ever slept in your life, and awaken refreshed and strengthened. Remember, the feeling you go to sleep with is the one you wake up with. When your mind is free as you go to sleep, powerful subconscious natural forces are free to work through you, refreshing and instructing your mind, developing your soul, and rebuilding your body.

There are no more valuable life tools than the Golden Bridge and its counterpart, the process of retrospection, by which you can go back over the events of your day in reverse order. When you practice these disciplines faithfully, you will rebuild your life completely. You will experience health, happiness, success, and fulfillment, because you will be constantly projecting them mentally, emotionally, and spiritually into your world.

This simple technique has changed my life. It came to me years ago when I was in meditation, just as I have explained it. I continue to use it every morning upon awakening and before I go to sleep each night. It sets my course for each day, each week, each month, each year, each decade, each century, each millennium, each lifetime, and for eternity. It helps me know where I am going and how to get there.

It has been my joy to share this valuable tool with countless numbers of students over the years, and now it is my privilege to share it with you. Please use it. It provides you with a foundation upon which to build the structure of your life. It is the framework upon which your plans and goals are formed. Build your Golden Bridge and travel across it from where you are to where you want to be.

THE SCIENCE AND ART OF GOAL-SETTING

Ask yourself the simple classic questions: Why am I here? What is the purpose of my life? What am I doing? Where am I going? As you ponder these questions through meditation and prayer, the answers will reveal themselves, a plan for your life will begin to emerge, and you will start to formulate some immediate and long-term goals.

Short-term goals have to do with the immediate, usually tangible and objective matters you are dealing with. The projected length of time will vary, for example, when you are setting goals of certain achievements such as increased income or professional advancement.

Long-term goals are more likely to deal with intangible and subjective factors, such as the kind of person you aspire to be, or spiritual growth, or overall well-being. However, some of your immediate, tangible goals may extend into a long-term goal projection.

In order to begin, you must know where you are going — or you will never get there. Would you try to build a house without a design and a detailed set of blueprints? Of course not! Neither can you build the most marvelous structure of all — your own life — without a master plan and purpose, and the goals that emanate from them.

The major part of your "work" is to make your plans and set your goals. Plans give rise to goals. Start right now where you are. If at first you can't get a clear picture of your goals, think about them, pray about them: *Father-Mother God, I know that you reveal to me what I am to do. I follow your guidance to the best of my ability as I seek to fulfill my life's purpose.*

Give your goal-setting a lot of thought. Divide your goals into two categories — short-term and long-term — and write down everything that presents itself, sifting and sorting both lists until you have pared them down to five definite immediate goals and five long-term ones. Memorize the lists or keep them handy to refer to and revise as you start building them, into your Golden Bridge.

You might prefer to simplify the process even more by just concentrating on three goals at a time in each category, then when one goal is completed replace it with another. Keep your priorities clearly in order, bringing all your goals together in thought, feeling, prayer, and action. You will find true achievement unfolding through you whether you know it or not.

As you do this faithfully your Golden Bridge will materialize, and you may travel upon it toward the fulfillment of your purpose. Do not delay. There is much to do, and you have the capacity to do it; do not be afraid to start, even though you may not be quite clear about everything. Set immediate goals and progress toward larger long-term goals as you go along. If you are not making satisfactory progress, examine your goals periodically. It may well be necessary for you to adjust them, realign them, or revise them completely. My goals and corresponding plans were changed several times before my life's purpose was revealed to me. Once that became clear, the Golden Bridge was given to me as the means of fulfilling it.

Use the cybernetic principle as explained so magnificently by Dr. Maxwell Maltz in his landmark book, *Psychocybernetics:*[1] Aim at the target. Within you is a self-adjusting principle that will keep moving you toward your objective and keep you on target, no matter how far off course you may be at any given time. The inner mechanism brings you back on course. Believe in it. Trust it. It is the will of God in you. We cannot escape our destiny, but remember, you are the master of your fate and the captain of your soul. You determine your own destiny. Travel the Golden Bridge toward fulfilling it. Knowing there is something important you are to do, knowing you are capable of doing it, and knowing its success is assured, is all the motivation you need.

Your personal use of the Golden Bridge gives you the consciousness of successful completion and achievement before you ever start. Daily practice in building your Golden Bridge strengthens your inner master plan and provides the mechanics for formulating your "game plan" for any given day or longer period of time. Since I know that I live forever, I build my Golden Bridge from now through infinity until forever. In other words, I have daily goals and plans; weekly, monthly, yearly, five-year, and ten-year plans; century plans, and many-lifetime plans, because I believe that I will be reincarnated many times.

---

[1] M. Maltz, *Psychocybernetics* (Englewood Cliffs, NJ: Prentice-Hall, 1960).

Just as a long, well-constructed bridge is an extension of many individual spans joined together, so is your eternal life an extension of the days for which you build the Golden Bridge. Today you are formulating a building block in your consciousness that not only structures this day but all the days to come, forever. This is why the "here and now" is so important. The Golden Bridge is the means by which you build the then, now.

Your Goals and Objectives

When you build your Golden Bridge each morning, visualize and affirm the completion of the goals you have for that day. Do the same for other periods of time for which you build your Golden Bridge. When you build for the longer periods— from a year to a lifetime—you will be setting forth long-term goals. Each evening, during your time of retrospection, check up on the day's progress of short-term goals, and periodically review your long-term goals, possibly revising or changing them in order to make even greater progress. Begin by grouping your goals and objectives into these classifications:

1) Personal Goals

2) Family Goals

3) Social Goals

4) Professional Goals

5) Financial Goals

6) Community Goals

7) Spiritual Goals

Personal Goals: What do you want to achieve in your life? What do you want to accomplish this year? What do you want to accomplish each day? What do you want to accomplish during your lifetime?

As you set your priorities, your goals, your objectives, your aims, your direction in life, think positively, think optimistically. Realize that you don't accomplish anything all by yourself. Yes, you are a self-starter, but as Jesus said, "I can of mine own self do nothing" (John 5:30). But God works through you to accomplish what you are to do. "With God all things are possible" (Matthew 19:26).

When you are choosing your personal goals and setting your objectives, be sure they are genuine. Be sure they are real. Don't get caught in the spurious appearances and superficiality of the outer world. You belong here, to learn and to do those things that need to be done by you, but you are not to be destroyed or consumed by the things of the world.

Family Goals: What are your goals for your family and your relationships within it? Are you giving the most and the best of yourself? Sometimes we give ourselves to everybody and everything else, but by the time we get home there is nothing left to give to our spouse or children or other family members. Sometimes our children go wanting for counsel, love, and instruction we could offer if we just took time to sit down and attempted to understand them.

In his radio program in the 1930s and 1940s, Father Peyton's slogan was "The family that prays together stays together." This is prayer in its larger scope—there must be communication between and among family members.

Husbands and wives must share together; they must communicate and share their feelings. Woman represents the soul of man; man represents the soul of woman. Together they make one whole unit. If marriage and family life are in your picture, you must have this kind of cooperation and mutual sharing. Not everyone lives in a family relationship. Some have never been married; some have been but are not married now. For some, the children have grown and moved away. For others, there has been a parting as a loved one moved into a larger sphere of expression. If you are single and alone, you must know there are many and wonderful examples of individuals who have been left alone who have full, vital, and wonderful lives of giving, expanding, and extending greater interests.

But the goals for all are the same. If yours is a family with a mother and father and a number of children, it is one kind of family unit. If it's a family with only a husband and wife together, it is another. If you are single, then you, yourself, are your family. You still have Father-Mother God; your thoughts and feelings are your children. Work it out by paying very close attention to your thoughts and feelings. Your thoughts are the soul to your feelings; your feelings are the soul to your thoughts.

The family lives in the home, and the home is the presence of God in your consciousness, where you are secure. It is where you go, where you communicate with God. It is where you have that inner sense of security and oneness.

Social Goals: Social goals are mutual goals with all your brothers and sisters in this great big, wide, wonderful world. People are gregarious creatures. They love to be together. If you are a person who is too much alone, too much withdrawn, too much introverted, you need to open your heart with love—open your consciousness to the "beingness" of other people. Be interested in them, share with them, communicate with them, learn from them, and love them.

You may say, "My tendency is to be alone; I am a loner. I like to do things by myself. I just like to get away by myself." Of course, there is a time to be alone. It is most necessary to "go into the closet" and talk with God, to find that inner sense of security and inner attunement and communication. But don't separate yourself from the human race. Balance. "In all things, moderation," said the ancient Greeks.

If you have loneliness in your life, if you feel that people pass you by and don't pay enough attention to you, it may be that you don't pay enough attention to others. If you have love, if you are interested in other people, if you are giving of yourself, people will give to you. But should you complain, whine, or indulge in self-pity, people stay away from you.

Take the first step. Be warm and outgoing. Have you ever said, "No one ever pays any attention to me. No one speaks to me"? How many people did you speak to on that particular day? How many greetings did you extend? How much did you smile? How pleasant was your manner? How did you act?

Get right inside yourself and realize that no one has it in for you. Fate, chance, and the law of averages have no power over you when you know truth. Don't blame anyone else for misfortune, failure, or lack of effectiveness. Don't blame yourself, either! Be realistic as you assess your thinking and how you feel about things. Thought and feeling come together to form conviction.

Thought comes first, then feeling. If you have fallen into habitual negative attitudes, take yourself in hand. Sit yourself down and have a talk with you. Set some positive goals for your social life.

Professional Goals: This is a more practical topic — you tend to pay close attention to your job, your business, and your creative endeavors. But you don't work just to make a living; you work to express yourself, to give what you have to give. And then life gives back what you need to sustain yourself: the necessities and conveniences and luxuries, as well.

If you are not happy in your job, take a good, long look at it and give it another month. Say to yourself: "I am going to give everything I have to this job; I am going to look for new ways to give and to be more effective." If you do that for one month, you will either fall in love with your job or you will move or be moved, easily, into something else.

Do your job to the best of your ability. Give everything you have to it. Make your work a true channel, a true avenue, for expressing yourself at your highest and best. Give of yourself, and you will put your stamp on your environment. As you set your professional goals, think in terms of what you can contribute to life, knowing that life will lavishly reward you in return.

Financial Goals: Be realistic about your financial goals. Someone has said, "I don't want too much money, just a little more than enough." Money is spiritual; money is God in action. Money is confirmation that you are doing something right. God has provided infinite abundance. If it is not flowing through your life, you cannot blame God—or circumstances, or other people. You cannot blame yourself, either, but it is necessary to develop a consciousness of abundance and love and giving. Develop a sense that the free, full flow of life is surging through you.

Comparisons are odious. Humans have a tendency to compare themselves with others: "His car is bigger than mine. He lives in a better house. He makes more money. He's up there in an executive position, I just work for a living." Isn't this rather ridiculous when you look at it closely? Why should you compare yourself with others, when all you can ever have, experience, or express is what comes to you by right of your own consciousness?

Build your consciousness of financial security by working on your inner feelings. First of all, get rid of any negative feelings that may be blocking you. Fear, anxiety, concern, worry, and tension must go. You may ask, "I know that, but how can I get rid of my worry and anxiety when they are caused by my financial problems?" Here's the answer: You can—if you want to, and if you will apply yourself. Dissolve your poor inner thoughts and feelings, and plant some constructive and creative ones. If you feel prosperous and secure inside, there is nothing that can keep you from becoming so.

Remember, your thoughts and feelings come first. Results always follow. What you are depends pretty much upon how you feel.

Feel prosperous. The clarity of your thought and the intensity of your feeling of prosperity will produce unlimited abundance in your life. The Creative Power within you produces the flow of money in your life according to the level of your consciousness.

Community Goals: As you formulate your goals, include everything that has to do with getting along with people in your community, whether it is one-to-one or in a group. These goals have to do with improving your neighborhood, your city, your county, your state. They have to do with the high goals of your country, and beyond that the international goal of peace on earth—and the universal cosmic goals to express the wonder, the glory, and the joy of God; the Kingdom of God on earth.

Spiritual Goals: Spiritual goals are always the overarching ones. Spirit is the oversoul of all. Set high spiritual goals. Find out more about God and experience Him; experience more of the Christ indwelling. Learn to experience more in meditation, prayer, and contemplation. Work to be more loving, work to give more, work to strengthen your inner consciousness. Learn to think positively; learn to be interested in other people. Everything is spirit if it is of good. If it is not of good, then it blocks spirit.

Realize what a wonderful person you are. God must love you very much to entrust you with His very life, because He has instilled within you the very essence of His being.

Let all the glamorous things of life happen to you as they will, if they happen. If they don't happen to you, don't be concerned. The real accomplishment, the real achievement, is to feel each day that you are doing the very best you can, giving everything you have to life on all levels. True achievement is bringing your thought, your prayer, your action, and your love all together into a blending of consciousness that becomes your contribution to life.

You are here to establish personal dominion, to develop what God has given you to develop. Some of us are bright lights, but some of us may not be shining brightly at the moment. Your potential, and mine, is infinite, but our experience in eternal life isn't identical—it is unique and different. Some of us are not as far along the path as others, but we do not know which are which. Perhaps those who appear to be the most ahead are the farthest back, while the simple and humble may be the most advanced, and teach us and lift us up with their quiet inner strength.

We are here in this world to live together, learn together, love together, grow together, and work together. Status in life has nothing to do with race, color, creed, distance or time. We live in the here and now. We are the human family; let us endeavor to work together and join together in a consciousness of good.

What a glorious opportunity! How inspiring it is to be on the front line every moment of life: to live every moment as though it were both the first and the last, to let the vital sweep of spirit move through you! Your failures and disappointments—even your hurts—are steps toward achievement if you capture their lessons and make them your own. Smile! Be cheerful, happy, and joyous! Sing! And take time for all the wonderful things that God provides. When you do, your achievement will be the expression of God in your life on every level and in all that you do. Take to heart the following poem by Rudyard Kipling:

> If you can keep your head when all about you
> Are losing theirs and blaming it on you,
> If you can trust yourself when all men doubt you,
> But make allowance for their doubting too;

If you can wait and not be tired by waiting,
Or, being lied about, don't deal in lies,
Or being hated don't give way to hating,
And yet don't look too good, nor talk too wise;

If you can dream — and not make dreams your
    master;
If you can think — and not make thoughts your aim,
If you can meet with Triumph and Disaster
And treat those two impostors just the same:
If you can bear to hear the truth you've spoken
Twisted by knaves to make a trap for fools,
Or watch the things you gave your life to, broken,
And stoop and build'em up with worn-out tools;

If you can make one heap of all your winnings
And risk it on one turn of pitch-and-toss,
And lose, and start again at your beginnings,
And never breathe á word about your loss:
If you can force your heart and nerve and sinew
To serve your turn long after they are gone,
And so hold on when there is nothing in you
Except the Will which says to them: "Hold on!"

If you can talk with crowds and keep your virtue,
Or walk with Kings — nor lose the common touch,
If neither foes nor loving friends can hurt you,
If all men count with you, but none too much:
If you can fill the unforgiving minute
With sixty seconds' worth of distance run,
Yours is the Earth and everything that's in it,
And — which is more — you'll be a Man, my son![2]

---

[2]R. Kipling, "If" in *One Hundred and One Famous Poems* (Chicago, IL: The Cable Co., 1929).

PERSONAL REALIZATION

The Infinite has stretched beckoningly before me as I build my Golden Bridge of harmony, Divine Order, and right action in my life. Today is my day. I live it fully and joyously. God's Infinite Law of Love flows through me; I am the channel of love and blessing through which all good things are expressed.

I know who I am and where I am going. I affirm my identity as a perfect expression of the Supreme Being, individualized in me. What is true of God is true of me. I have infinite potential. I have unlimited possibilities. I give thanks for harmony, balance, and proper action in my life, now and forever.

My Golden Bridge of high consciousness spans this day, this week, this month, this year, and my entire life throughout eternity. I am an eternal being, living each moment fully and abundantly.

My goals unfold in accordance with my life's purpose and my plans for fulfilling it. I keep on track. I move steadily forward. I am clear and definite in setting my short-term goals, and I develop expanded spiritual vision and high consciousness in the formation of my long-term goals. I keep ever before me the image of what I am and what I can become. I work steadily to do that which God has given me to do, and to be that which God has created me to be.

As I follow the path of spiritual development, my personality reflects the true nature of my inner being, and cooperates with me in all matters concerning purpose, plans, and goals. I grow in effectiveness as I develop the areas in my consciousness where I am weak. In so doing, I attain balance, harmony, and maturity. I follow that inner compass of my Higher Self, which indicates to me the direction in which I should go.

I am on my way into glorious achievement as I stay upon my soundly structured Golden Bridge forever. And so it is. Thank You, Father-Mother God.

CHAPTER 6

GIVE THANKS FOR EVERYTHING

Start now to give thanks for everything in your life. That means everything—whether you consider it good or not. Everything is part of your life. You love your life, so give thanks for everything. An attitude of gratitude is the most constructive foundation for your life you can possibly have. Giving thanks for the good things expands and increases them, while giving thanks for the less desirable aspects suspends and neutralizes them so that you may have an opportunity to analyze and deal with them.

As you pursue a policy of "bless, praise and curse not," you will often find that even a disastrous situation may be a blessing in disguise. Your attitude toward the challenge is the most important factor in meeting it constructively. Say—and mean: *Thank You, Father-Mother God, for this evidence of Thy love for me. Through this means do I grow.*

Of course, you don't invite disaster. But if it comes, turn it to your advantage. Make an asset out of it. Your attitude of gratitude helps this happen. Thanksgiving is "thanksliving."

In giving thanks to God, I say "Father-Mother God," rather than the traditional (in our Western Judeo-Christian tradition) "Father." "Father-Mother God" is used in Hinduism and in many other spiritual traditions, but "Father" has come down through Judaism and Christianity because of patriarchal tradition and, until recent times, male dominated society. (Actually, male chauvinism continues to hang on, even though it makes no sense.) All creatures must have two parents. To call God "Father," alone, is to ignore the female aspect of our parentage. The "Father" is the male, active principle. The "Mother" is the creative, love principle. "Male and female created he them" (Genesis 1:27). The male and the female (active and creative) principles are active in every one of us. When we say, "Father-Mother God," we are recognizing and affirming the dual unity of the reality we know as God.

If you are comfortable saying, "Thank You, Father-Mother God," then do so by all means. It has a powerful effect upon your inner consciousness, as long as you realize that God is within you. You are not praying *to* anything. You are affirming the healing activity of God as the only reality in your life.

The same approach applies if you say, "In the Name and through the Power of Jesus Christ." You may or may not wish to end your affirmative period with this phrase, depending upon your formal religious conditioning or orientation. However, by making this statement, you elevate your consciousness to a higher level of causative significance. "In the Name" means "in the nature." "Jesus" means the recognition of the perfect potential within you. "Christ" is the perfection of God in you. So what you actually mean as you say these two seemingly formal religious phrases is, *I am grateful that the Infinite Reality responds to my gratitude and activates its perfection through me, freeing me from mortal limitations, and restoring me to my natural state of fulfilled potential.*

As you begin the process of changing your life by giving thanks, keep a pencil and note pad with you at all times to jot down what your inner teacher and companion is telling you. The personal notebook is a very important factor in your self-discovery and self-unfoldment. Never, never be without something to write on! Your notes will tell you, over a period of time, everything you need to know about yourself, and, eventually, everything else.

Always keep a pencil and pad on your bedside table at night. Your dreams are a tremendous source of instruction. Jot them down and meditate upon them upon awakening. Ideas will come to you during your sleep that may be very important to you. Just awaken enough to write them down. Plans, projects, and solutions to problems are constantly coming up from your subconscious while you are asleep; the subconscious continues to work—whether you are awake or asleep—on whatever it is that your conscious mind is involved with, until you tell it to stop. (Don't ever tell it to stop. It is a loyal, resourceful friend.) Your ever-present notebook is a record of your relationship with your subconscious mind.

My pencil and pad are with me day and night, awake or asleep. Much of the material for this book, just as for my more than twenty other books, was developed from notes that I have taken at odd times, some of them many years ago.

You may say, "Oh, I don't want to bother with writing things down. It's too much trouble and it just creates clutter. I'll just remember what I need to know." But I adjure you, try it! It will free your mind for tasks at hand, and it will be one of your best sources of guidance and information. Right now, form the habit of carrying a personal notebook.

I cannot remember when I first discovered the importance of my personal notebook, but I am sure it was when I was just a child. Very early in my life I had a dream of becoming a writer. During the long, lonely days in the farm fields, I would work out elaborate plots upon which some day my novels would be based. Well, as it worked out, this particular material never saw print, but the notebook habit was firmly established, and continues to provide me with a steady stream of material for classes, lectures, sermons, articles, and books.

Much of what you are reading right now was developed from notes jotted down in my personal notebook, many of them during the night.

Whenever you are engaged in peripheral activity of any kind, your subconscious mind is very active, and you need to have your notebook with you to capture its communication. For instance, when I am watching TV or listening to music, I receive a steady stream of ideas and instructions from my subconscious. Along with God, my subconscious is my best friend. Yours is your best friend, too. Do it the honor of listening to it and remembering what it says by keeping your personal notebook with you, ready for use.

The basic material for one of the chapters in this book was worked out fully while I was watching a movie in a theater. I continued to watch the picture peripherally, and at the same time wrote rapidly in my notebook as the chapter unfolded from my subconscious. I had to be ready to capture what my inner friend was giving. My two books of poetry, *Songs of the Soul* and *Cosmic Awareness,* were compiled from poems that came to me at various times and during various activities—driving, walking, sailing, gardening, playing golf—over a period of several years. My notebook helps me capture my thoughts and hold them for me until I can do something with them. Your notebook will help you do the same. Remember, your thoughts build and change your life.

YOUR THANKFUL LISTS

Here are four lists for you to make in developing your consciousness of thanksgiving as an ongoing way of life:

1) All the wonderful things in your life.

2) Undesirable and unhappy situations in your life.

3) All your good points.

4) All your character traits that should be changed.

While you are making these lists, give thanks for each item as you write it down. The process of giving thanks will release the full potential of the item for which you are showing your appreciation, and it will lead you onward to an awareness and discovery of new areas that you are grateful for, but had not really thought about.

The Wonderful Things: No item is too large or too small for you to be grateful for. Get a long pad of yellow paper and a good pen or pencil and start writing. Don't think about it too much; just let it flow, and put down whatever items come into your mind, saying as you write, "Thank You, Father-Mother God, for my life. Thank You for my family. Thank You for my wife or husband. Thank You for my children. Thank You for nature. Thank You for the Sun, the Moon and the stars." Never stop. As you write down each item, say, "I give thanks for _____" or, "Thank you, Father-Mother God, for _____."

Keep this up for as long as you can, writing and speaking at the same time. This process is an ongoing, positive prayer of thanksgiving. It will make you a permanently positive person. You cannot be thankful and negative at the same time. The more you give thanks, the more you have to be thankful for. Since thoughts are things and consciousness is the only reality, your gratitude becomes the cause of your experience, and you can experience only good in your life.

As your list lengthens, you will probably find that you do not have time to complete it at any one sitting. Wonderful! This shows that the process of giving thanks is working. Before leaving the list, go back over it, repeating, "Thank You, Father-Mother God" for each item. Then put it aside and go on about your business. However, you will realize that your list is not yet complete (actually, it never will be), so be prepared to jot down additional thanksgiving items to add to your master list. Keep accumulating these items.

From time to time, go over the entire list, giving thanks once again for each item. If at any time during your day you become discouraged or upset or negative in any way, take a few minutes to give thanks out loud, until you are back on track again. Giving thanks is true affirmative prayer. It increases the good in your life.

Prayer is not for the purpose of coercing God's givingness, but of preparing your own receptivity. Do not pray to God for things, or ask Him for anything. He has already given you everything; it only remains for you to prepare your consciousness to receive. Thanksgiving enables you to do so.

"Your Father knoweth what things ye have need of, before ye ask him" (Matthew 6:8).

"It is your Father's good pleasure to give you the kingdom" (Luke 12:32).

"What things soever ye desire, when ye pray, believe that ye receive them, and ye shall have them" (Mark 11:24).

True prayer is not asking; it is affirming. Thanksgiving (giving thanks) is the ultimate affirmation. Whatever you affirm, believing, you must receive and experience. Expressing complete gratitude is all you ever need to do in your prayer. Your prayer is purely a personal matter; it is about you, and it all takes place within you. Your prayer does not do anything to God, who is already whole and complete, but it does a great deal to you, because you (as all of us do) have a long way to go. Giving thanks provides the momentum that moves you out of separation into union with God where there is no place where He leaves off and you begin. The prayer of thanksgiving unifies you with the abundance of life.

You need no other prayer in addition to your affirmations of thanksgiving. One of your affirmations may well be, *Thank You, God, for being God,* but you don't really pray *to* God. You pray as an action of God taking place within your own consciousness. God is omnipresent; there is no place where He is not. Since you are one with God, there is no place where you are not (in consciousness). Your prayer of thanksgiving affirms that this is so. That is all you need in order to live life abundantly. Jesus said, "I am come that they might have life, and that they might have it more abundantly" (John 10:10). The "I" is your attitude of gratitude. This brings you the abundant life on every level.

Give thanks each morning upon arising for all the good in your life. Affirm, both specifically and generally. Let your praise, blessing, and appreciation pour out from your heart. Sing! Shout! Jump with joy! Let the positive energies of praise and blessing vibrate through your entire being, spiritually, mentally, emotionally, physically, and materially.

I combine part of my thanksgiving affirmations with my morning exercise period and as I walk and jog, shouting and singing: *"Thank You, Father-Mother God! Thank You, Father-Mother God!"* I make a free-flowing chant out of it, and spend time on whatever areas in my life may need the positive attention of praise, blessing, and thanksgiving. This works wonders for me, and I know it will for you. It works, but remember, you have to do it.

Express particular gratitude for good you desire, which has not yet manifested in your experience. Your thanksgiving establishes a positive acceptance in your consciousness and activates the creative process that produces the desired good. You establish dominion in your own life, and control your own destiny, by building an inner conviction that you already have your desired good before it actually appears. Giving thanks is the means by which this conviction is established and maintained.

After your early morning period of thanksgiving, carry your high positive consciousness with you throughout the day. If you bog down, repeat the process. First, get clearly in mind what you want to be and do. Second, develop a strong conviction that it is already accomplished. The more you consciously practice this technique, the stronger and longer will be your positive periods, and the more good will appear in your life.

Repeat the thanksgiving process just before you go to sleep at night. This will be part of your Golden Bridge retrospection process. After a period of quiet thanksgiving, you will be ready to drop off to sleep with a peaceful sense of well-being. The creative forces of spirit will work throughout the night to produce what you have accepted through thanksgiving as being already true in your experience.

Undesirable and Unhappy Situations: In your first list, you recognize the good things that are already extant in your life and give thanks for them. In this second list you are not giving thanks for the actual problems, difficulties, or illnesses themselves—you are not really happy or grateful for them! But you realize from experience that if you complain, resist, or condemn them, they get worse. Your prayer of thanksgiving concerning the items on this list reverses your consciousness so that you affirm the good instead of the negative condition or appearance. Again, this is the process of giving thanks for the good before it appears. Remember, your inner consciousness is always cause. Your attitude about the outer, undesirable effect that has appeared determines whether it stays as it is, gets worse, or is healed.

The "I," as we have seen, is the healing power of your attitude of gratitude. Inherent in this process is the dissolving of the negativity in your consciousness, which brought about (or at least, contributed to) the illness or problem in the first place. Remember, where the problem seems to be, God is already there. There may be secondary negative causes in these instances, but if you assume that you can contribute to the healing or the solution by building constructive causation within your consciousness, then you are in charge of the situation. Giving thanks for the healing, even in the face of the situation, is the way you do it.

Go over each item on this list. As you write down the undesirable situation that needs to be dealt with, take time to say affirmations of gratitude that the cause of the problem is dissolved, and that the healing has already taken place. Speak that conviction out loud for each situation:

Thank You, Father-Mother God, that this situation is dissolved and that complete healing has already taken place. Anything and everything unlike the nature of God is dissolved from my consciousness. All fear and concern are dissolved. I give thanks for this challenge as the means by which I overcome evil with good, and experience the full, free flow of life throughout every level of my being. I am filled with joy and gratitude. I experience God's healing activity in every aspect of my consciousness and in every part of my body and world of experience. I give thanks for complete healing, now. Thank You, Father-Mother God. In the Name and through the Power of Jesus Christ. And so it is.

Take inventory of your entire life as you make this second list. Don't go looking for things that are wrong; but if you are dealing with something in your life that is not right, write it down and work on it with the thanksgiving, praise, and blessing technique. Do not ignore it or neglect it, because you have the power within you to correct and heal it. Remember, whenever an undesirable situation appears in your life, it is for a reason. This reason is to reveal to you that some corrections need to be made within yourself, and that you have the power within you to heal whatever it is. You are never confronted with anything you cannot handle. You can handle anything and everything that comes your way.

Say to yourself (aloud if convenient): "It came to pass. It did not come to stay. It came to pass." Then, help it pass out of your experience by developing attitudes of gratitude for the solution, change, and healing that have come about. In this way, you become co-creator with God of your own life. As you practice the discipline of supplanting negative attitudes with affirmative ones, thanksgiving will become your way of life. Your second list will become shorter and shorter, and your first list will become longer and longer. The ultimate, of course, is to always be thankful for everything. You are now ready to make a list of all your good points.

Your Good Points: Be honest with yourself. You have many, many good points. There is unlimited good within. That good is expressing itself through you right now, or you would not be here. Do not be timid about making this list and giving thanks for your good points. You are not being egotistical — if you don't recognize the good in you, no one else is going to. Jesus instructed, "Love thy neighbour as thyself" (Matthew 22:39). You can't love anyone unless you first love yourself.

Your "self" is what you are. Give thanks for yourself, and dedicate your life to making yourself better. Do this by using the praise, blessing, and thanksgiving technique. As you list each good characteristic, quality, or ability, give thanks for it: *Thank You, Father-Mother God, for all of my good qualities. I am thankful for my honesty. I am grateful for my integrity. I give thanks for my dependability. I praise my persistence* . . . The list can be endless, just as it is when you make the list of all the things you have to be thankful for.

When you give thanks, you increase and expand what you are thankful for. You are strengthening and increasing your good qualities when you recognize and bless them. Be thorough in making this list. Examine every part of your consciousness in your search for your good points.

You have many good qualities that you don't even know you have until you look for them. This is an adventure in self-discovery. You will find that you are a wonderful person, with qualities and potentials far beyond anything you ever dreamed of. The step of giving thanks for all your good points is totally constructive, just as all thanksgiving is. It dissolves all doubts and fears. It builds your self-esteem. It makes you comfortable with yourself, and confident that you can be and do anything you set your mind to.

As you are making your list, speak your affirmations about each good point as you write it down. Take time to develop it fully. Make the good points you are recognizing and discovering a permanent part of your being. Just as in your previous lists, continue to build your inventory of good qualities.

As you are making the list of all of your good qualities, including the ones you have searched for and the ones you discovered that you didn't know you had, move into the area of desirable qualities and traits you would like to have, but have not yet developed. Give thanks that you have them. Remember the importance of this technique. Give thanks for your desired good as being an already accomplished fact in your experience, before it actually appears.

You have learned to do this in demonstrating health, prosperity, and achievement in your life; now give thanks for qualities that you would like to have but have not yet developed in your life. For instance, you might want to be a warm, loving, outgoing individual, but you are actually shy, timid, and withdrawn. Change your life by adding to your list of good points, "I am a warm, loving, outgoing person." Repeat this affirmation over and over until you start to believe it. As soon as you start to believe it, you will begin to act like it. This is how your thoughts change your life.

Move along now to other desirable qualities you would like to have but don't at this moment. For instance, you want to be cheerful and joyous, but you tend to be morose and depressed. Add to your "good" list: "I am cheerful and joyous," and give thanks that you are, even though up to now you may not have been.

Keep at it. Compile the list of your good points by recognizing the ones you have, and including the ones you want to have but have not developed up to this point. Now give thanks that you *do* have them. Convince yourself that you really do, and you really will. Keep building the list of good points you want to develop.

Use your thoughts to transform yourself into the person you want to be by giving thanks that you already are. Paul said, "Be ye transformed by the renewing of your mind" (Romans 12:2). The greatest way to renew your mind is to give thanks for the good stuff that is in it, or that you now put in it by the conscious choice of your own personal will. When you make that choice and give thanks for it, your subconscious mind accepts it and makes it true. Your subconscious mind does not know the difference between a fact and something simply imaged vividly and in detail. Giving thanks is the best way of imaging what is not yet true, but should be.

Your Undesirable Character Traits: As you embark upon a program of personal spiritual growth, it will be obvious that some things about yourself need to be changed. There may be flaws in character and disposition that need to be corrected. No one can accomplish this but you.

The first step is to recognize each flaw, one at a time, and admit that you have it. This may not be easy to do, because your personal ego has a tendency to defend you just the way you are, no matter what. However, it also takes pride in your being the best person you can possibly be. Therefore, it is up to you to recognize that your faults are keeping you from being what you can be and accomplishing what you are capable of. Once you realize this is true, your second step is to set about changing what needs to be changed. This is where thanksgiving comes in.

List each fault; and beside it, the virtue which is its opposite. Here are some examples:

Fault	Virtue
Rude	Polite
Thoughtless	Thoughtful
Inconsiderate	Considerate
Mean	Kind
Sarcastic	Sincere

Vicious	Gentle
Boorish	Interesting
Lazy	Energetic
Bored	Enthusiastic
Loud	Soft-spoken
Hateful	Loving
Self-effacing	Confident

Do you see how it works? Keep at it, continuously fine-tuning yourself. Recognize and list your undesirable characteristics, decide to change them, and then go about changing them into virtues—just the opposite of what they are now. The reason there are so many unpleasant characters in the world is that either they don't know, they don't care, or they are too lazy to do anything about it. None of these attitudes is good enough for you. Get rid of any fault by giving thanks for the virtue ahead of time. This will establish the virtue in your subconscious mind, and it will then become true.

Here is an example. We'll change "meanness" into "kindness": *All meanness is dissolved from my disposition as I free my consciousness from anything unlike the nature of God. All meanness is dissolved, and I become kind and loving. I give thanks that I am a kind and loving person. I am thankful that I am always loving and kind to others. I speak words of kindness, and I do kind and helpful things. I give thanks for the wonder and beauty of other people, and I praise and bless the virtues within me that make me a kind and loving person, now and from now on. And so it is.*

Take time to follow this procedure for every one of your character faults. Keep at it, and repeat the affirmations, giving thanks for the desired virtue until you get results. You will start to feel different inside, and, as a result, you will start to act differently. You will suit the action to the word, the word to the action. By giving thanks for your desired good quality, that quality expands and develops until it completely replaces the previous fault. The principle always works. You are in complete charge of yourself and your life when you give thanks for your desired good as being an already established fact in your experience, before it actually appears. Your feeling of gratitude is the cause that produces the desired effect.

The kingdom of heaven is within you. Praise, gratitude, blessing, thanksgiving, and appreciation expand your consciousness, thereby increasing the good in your experience. The kingdom of expansion is within you. Keep expanding your consciousness by giving thanks.

"A mind expanded to the dimensions of a greater idea can never return to its original size." Thanksgiving is "a greater idea." It expands your mind permanently, into new and larger dimensions; therefore, you are in a "heavenly" state. Heaven is a state of mind. Thanksgiving is "thanksliving"—a way of life. Make thanksgiving your way of life.

From the basis of what you have accomplished by making these four lists and using thanksgiving as the technique for achieving desired good, you now see how giving thanks is a most valuable tool for changing your thoughts and thereby changing your life.

THE HEALING POWER OF THANKSGIVING

Praise, blessing, and thanksgiving quicken the vibrations in your consciousness and in your body. Your body is your thoughts, feelings, and attitudes in tangible, physical form. When illness or disease appear in your body, it is the result of negative causation in your consciousness. Therefore, in order to be healed, it is necessary to change your consciousness.

Your thoughts change your life. Thoughts of thanksgiving heal; there is great healing power in thanksgiving. Whatever indisposition, pain, or malfunction you may be experiencing, start right now to give thanks for the healing of the condition, and for the restoration of full and perfect health: *I give thanks that anything and everything unlike the nature of God is dissolved from my consciousness and from my physical body right now. I am grateful that I am organically and functionally whole. I give thanks for perfect circulation, perfect assimilation, and perfect elimination on every level of my being, including the physical. I am grateful that the free, full flow of life is surging through my mind and my body, healing me and making me whole. My heart is beating in rhythm with the heart of the Universe. Every drop of my blood is filled with the elixir of abundant life. Every cell of my body is revolving in a clockwise direction, manifesting the pure and perfect expression of Spirit. I give thanks for the complete healing that has already taken place in my body and is permanently sustained and maintained. I am healed. I am whole. Thank You, Father-Mother God, for my complete and perfect health. In the Name and through the Power of Jesus Christ. And so it is.*

Repeat this affirmative treatment of thanksgiving for your healing until you reach full inner realization, which will be followed by the physical healing in the flesh and function of your body. This is the process of building your faith through giving thanks that your healing has already taken place and there is nothing to heal. To the extent that you can completely reach this state of faith in your complete wholeness, the outer healing will take place. Jesus said, "Thy faith hath made thee whole" (Mark 10:52).

This is the technique of healing through prayer. The basis of true scientific prayer is building the acceptance of the desired good through praise, blessing, and thanksgiving. During my many years of professional practice of these principles, I have experienced countless numbers of healings in my own body and in my world of affairs through the use of affirmative, thanksgiving prayer, and I have helped many others experience healing through this means.

I say "helped" advisedly, because no one ever heals himself or anyone else. The healing comes about because of the change of consciousness within the individual. The person may accomplish it by his own prayer, or it may be through the prayer assistance of a friend, practitioner, counselor, or minister. The principle is always the same: "All things whatsoever ye shall ask in prayer, believing, ye shall receive" (Matthew 21:22).

This applies to physical healing as well as healing on every other level. But the healing is never done *to* you; it is done *through* you. Nor is it done by anyone or anything other than your acceptance of wholeness in your own consciousness. This wholeness in consciousness is called "the Father" by Jesus.

Does the healing always take place? Of course not. You know it and I know it. Why not? Because the conditions have not been met to build the inner consciousness of wholeness. Perhaps doubt and fear are still there. Any negative in one's consciousness blocks the good and delays the healing. I do not always experience healing in myself or for those with and for whom I pray, but this does not keep me from giving thanks that the healing has already taken place. I refuse to relinquish this belief, for I know that what is within me is greater than what is in the world. I continually give thanks for this inner power (the "Father"), and you must do so also if you would experience healing and the demonstration of good in your world.

Keep on giving thanks for everything. I give thanks every day, as I have in some instances for many years, for the healing of certain conditions in my body, sometimes with absolutely no noticeable results whatsoever. But I have not abandoned my prayers of thanksgiving that the condition is healed. I know that sooner or later, one by one, complete healings will come about. Wouldn't it be a pity if any one of us stopped our thanksgiving healing prayers too soon, just because the healing hadn't taken place when we thought it should from our limited personal human point of view? The Bible says, "A thousand years in thy sight are but as yesterday when it is past, and as a watch in the night" (Psalms 90:4).

In case you have doubts or questions about healing through prayer and thanksgiving, perhaps this hypothetical question and answer session will clear them up:

Question: Does this mean there is a possibility that I might not accomplish my healing during this lifetime? That I might die from my ailment?

Answer: Yes, that is a possibility. That is the way it happens in some cases.

Question: Then why should I pray and give thanks for the healing having already taken place, if it is not going to happen anyway?

Answer: Your question is most understandable. But remember, you cannot pray with thanksgiving without healing taking place. It just might not be completely manifested in this lifetime.

Question: Then what good is it?

Answer: You don't know how much worse the condition might get if you don't pray and give thanks for the healing. And remember, no good is ever lost; no sincere prayer of praise, blessing, and thanksgiving ever goes unanswered.

Question: But you said the healing might not come about in this lifetime.

Answer: Yes, but this lifetime is only a tiny segment of your complete life, which is continuous and goes on forever. Therefore, any good that is accomplished during this short span—even up to the two hundred years or more that will soon be a reasonable life expectancy—will accrue and manifest during your eternal life. Jesus called this "Laying up treasures in heaven" (Matthew 6:20).

The best way is to meet whatever comes your way with fortitude, purpose, prayer, and thanksgiving, and have no concern as to the outcome. If the healing comes, it comes; if not, you may have accomplished something greater, without realizing it. The important thing is to sustain praise, blessing, and thanksgiving as your way of life.

Question: What about medical assistance? Should I go to the doctor during this time when I am praying and waiting for healing to take place?

Answer: That's up to you. But continue your healing prayers, giving thanks that the healing has already taken place. This will reinforce the medical treatment. God is in the doctor, but don't expect the doctor, or the medicine, or possible surgery to heal you. The healing must come from within yourself. The doctor may help it take place. Work in cooperation with the doctor, but do not concentrate upon the condition; focus upon the healing, and continue to know that you are whole, strong and healthy. Give thanks that it is so, and go on about your business.

BLESS YOUR BODY

Do not wait for illness or pain before starting to praise, bless, and give thanks for your strong and healthy body. Every day, focus your attention upon every organ and function of your body, giving thanks that it is whole and perfect. This is the best conditioning and preventative medicine there is. It keeps your body well and in good functioning order. It isn't just that there is a relationship between your mind and your body. Your body is your mind in physical expression. The Greeks said, "A sound mind in a sound body."

Be your own physician. Be your own therapist. Be your own masseur or masseuse. Love your body. Praise it and bless it. Thank your body for what it is and what it does for you. It will respond and do its very best to serve you. Give attention to your entire body, with specific attention to every part of it. Proceed as follows: *I give thanks for my strong, vital, and*

*beautiful body. I give thanks for perfect circulation, perfect
assimilation, and perfect elimination. I am grateful for my
heart, which beats in rhythm with the heart of the Universe.
Thank You, Father-Mother God, for the Life force circulat-
ing through my body. I give thanks for the vital energy of
pure being that animates me.*

Continue this affirmation, giving thanks for all the systems and organs and functions, until you have covered your
entire body. This takes some time, but when you measure its
benefits against some of the useless things you (and all of us)
spend time doing, it will all come into perspective. How
much time might be spent if you became seriously ill because
you neglected your body, while all the time this simple practice of praise, blessing, and thanksgiving could have been
maintaining you in perfect health? As the sign in the busy
shop asks, "If you don't have time to do it right, do you have
time to do it over?"

Time

Time has many faces:
Good time
Bad time
Idle time
Busy time
Dull time
Happy time
Noisy time
Quiet time.

This I know:
I do have time to do
All the things
God has given me to do,
So I take time to do them.
I live in God's time.[1]

---

[1]D. Curtis, "Time" in *Songs of the Soul* (Lakemont, GA: CSA Press, 1979), p. 95.

SOLVING PROBLEMS

Use the same praise, blessing, thanksgiving technique to straighten out the problem areas that arise in your life. The important thing, first of all, is to not get upset when problems arise. You will always have problems because it is through solving them that you grow. When a problem or difficulty arises, always say, *Thank You, Father-Mother God, for this evidence of Thy love for me. Through this means do I grow.* When you give thanks for the problem, you take all negative energy away from it, and it becomes your friend, rather than your enemy.

The teaching is, "resist not evil" (Matthew 5:39), "but overcome evil with good" (Romans 12:21). In giving thanks for problems and difficulties, you activate the creative power of God in the situation. "If God be for us, who can be against us?" (Romans 8:31). By giving thanks for the problem, you open your mind to learn from it, thereby getting the greatest good out of the experience. Use this technique, and you will never rail and rant against outrageous fortune again.

Giving thanks for the problem is the essential first step, but it is only the beginning. Now, give thanks for the solution—for the healing of the situation. Know that where the problem seems to be, God is already there. Give thanks for the situation the way you want it to be, accept it as being already true, and praise and bless the order and corrective action that are taking place.

Follow this procedure whenever a challenge comes up in your life, and you will grow and grow. When you give thanks for the problem, its power becomes your power to create a solution. When you give thanks for the solution, it is amplified and multiplied into ever-expanding greater good.

Just as you do in healing your body and establishing wholeness (health) in every cell by praising, blessing, and giving thanks, go over every area of your life: spiritual, mental, emotional, physical, material, professional, social, financial, experiential, and creative, giving thanks for and praising the good that is taking place there. Remind yourself why and how this works. It is not that your affirmations and prayers of praise, blessing, and thanksgiving do anything to the outer aspects of your life. They don't. But they do change the thoughts, feelings, and attitudes that form your consciousness, which is the cause of your experience. Change your consciousness and your life changes.

Expanding Your Talents and Abilities

In the first list, giving thanks for all your good points, I am sure you included your many talents and abilities. If you didn't, take a complete inventory of them now and add them to your gratitude list. Make a special list of these talents and abilities, and start to praise, bless, and give thanks for each one. As you do this, you will find that you have many more than you realized. We all have a tendency to underestimate our talents and abilities.

Reverse this tendency by giving thanks, praising, and blessing the talents and abilities you know you have. Look for others you did not know you had, and start to develop them by the same method. You will be gratified to find that your sphere of activity will expand and your level of performance will be greatly enhanced. You never know what you can do until you try, and you can do whatever you make up your mind to do. Nothing is too good to be true. Nothing is too wonderful to happen. Celebrate yourself by praising, blessing, and giving thanks for your talents and abilities.

Goal Achievement

Throughout the book, we come back to your goals, plans, and objectives—how to set them and how to achieve them. By now, you realize that the only way to achieve anything is to give thanks that it is an already established fact in your experience. In this way, your goals, dreams, and plans become tangible reality. Just as you have used the praise, blessing, and thanksgiving technique to bring health to your body and to solve problems and overcome difficulties, now go over your goals and plans, praise them and bless them, and give thanks that they are already fulfilled. The importance of following this procedure regularly and thoroughly cannot be stressed too much. That is why I repeat it over and over again.

Build the inner structure and the outer structure will appear by the natural process of the creative law of nature working through you.

Personal Realization

I love life and I love to live. I give thanks for everything. Thank You, Father-Mother God, for Life and the privilege of living it. Thank You for Truth and the wonder of knowing it. Thank You for Light and the brightness of it. Thank You for Love and the thrill of giving and receiving it. Thank You for Intelligence and the opportunity to use it. Thank You for Beauty and the capacity to perceive it. Thank You for Joy and the ebullient expression of it. Thank You for People and the blessing of knowing them. Thank You for Work and the fulfillment of doing it. Thank You, Father-Mother God, for being God.

I am grateful for this great, big, wide, beautiful world in which I live. I give thanks for the expanse of it and for the freshness and beauty of it. I am nurtured at the breast of my Mother Earth. I drink deeply from the wellsprings of the Spirit. My cup runneth over.

As the Universe reveals itself to me, I am grateful for the Sun, the Moon, and the Stars. I praise the beauty of the orbiting planets and heavenly bodies. The Milky Way fills me with awe and wonder. I give thanks for the constellations and the galaxies, which uplift and inspire me.

My soul flies free into the limitless expanses of outer space, up into the sky and beyond. I am at home in the timeless, spaceless reality of the Cosmos. I give thanks for my eternal being. I am a native of Eternity. I am a Cosmic being. I am a child of the Universe. I give thanks to God in whom I live and move and have my being. I am grateful for God's arms forever around me.

"I can do all things through Christ which strengtheneth me" (Philippians 4:13). *I give thanks for "Christ in [me], [my] hope of glory"* (Colossians 1:27). *I give thanks for the glorious panoply of pure being which surrounds and protects me.*

I give thanks for my expanding consciousness. I am grateful for my thoughts, which change my life. I give thanks for awareness and perception. I give thanks for wisdom and understanding. I give thanks for vision and insight. I give thanks for intuition and enlightenment. I know, and I am grateful that I know.

Thank You, Father-Mother God, for the talents and abilities You have given me. Thank You for the inspiration to keep striving and growing. Thank You for the creative drive that surges through my life. Thank You for work and the driving will to do it. Thank You for the privilege of doing Your Will in helping and serving others. Thank You for using me to fulfill Your purposes. I am grateful for the opportunity to give myself totally and unconditionally to bring about total peace on earth and good will among men.

CHAPTER 7

FORWARD! ONWARD! UPWARD!

Since the Greek word for *heaven* (*ouranos*) is also used for *expansion,* we can surmise that "heaven" is an expanded state of growth that everyone is constantly moving toward. Evolution by itself is always working to bring about the perfection of the species.

When Jesus instructs, "Be ye therefore perfect, even as your Father which is in heaven is perfect" (Matthew 5:48), He is setting out for humanity the necessity of moving ever forward, upward, and inward toward the ultimate that is our destiny. There is good etymological evidence to support the position that the correct translation of this passage is actually, "You *are* perfect, even as your Father in heaven is perfect." In this case, it means that you are created whole and perfect, but given freedom of choice and left on your own to determine if, when, and how this ultimate goal is to be achieved.

The Voyage

Living, loving, laughing, learning,
All aboard for the voyage of life!
The sails are full and trim
As I embark for the distant shore.

My hand is firm on the wheel,
My eye is trained on the Star,
My heart beats with the swelling tide,
And deep beckons to deep.

I may not know where I am going,
I may often be lost in the night,
But the Spirit carries me in
Its loving arms and the days are calm and bright.

Forward, onward, inward and upward I grow,
Untouched by the shallows and storms.
I am in charge of my ship and my crew,
And God brings me safely to port.

The tests are never easy,
Nor the challenges casual or light,
But sailing onward day and night,
We complete the voyage of life.[1]

It is impossible to stand still without atrophying, deterio-
rating, and dying. Therefore, you actually have no choice but
to cooperate with life and direct all of your energies toward
moving ever forward, onward, and upward. As Ernest
Holmes used to say in his lectures, "We're all hell-bent for
heaven by way of evolution." We must have a philosophy of
moving better up to best, and of hitching our wagons to stars.
It is not a matter of if or why; it is one of when (now) and
how.

I am richly blessed in having been highly motivated by
my mother and father, who always expected my brother and
sisters and me to be top achievers. The four of us apparently
came into this life with high motivation, and the high demands and expectations of our parents served to heighten,

---

[1]D. Curtis, "The Voyage" in *Songs of the Soul,* p. 54.

reinforce, and strengthen the ascending tide that was already strong within us. If I ever got discouraged, my parents were always there to remind me that I had greatness within me, and could do whatever I set out to do. I already believed that, and when my mother would remind me of it, it gave me a tremendous impetus forward, onward, and upward.

Jesus taught, "If two of you shall agree on earth as touching any thing that they shall ask, it shall be done for them of my Father which is heaven" (Matthew 18:19). I am sure all of us who have been encouraged and inspired by our mothers can understand how Abraham Lincoln felt when he said that whatever he was or ever hoped to be, he owed to his angel mother. I still frequently use a little chant that we used to repeat when we were all working together on some difficult farm task. My mother would always get it started.

> Good, better, best,
> Never let it rest,
> 'Til the good is better,
> And the better best.

We would join in and keep it up for several minutes, going faster and faster until we finally fell in a heap, laughing. And you know something, often the task at hand was completed with much less difficulty, and we were all eager to direct our energy to the next one.

There is a tremendous power in doing well whatever you have to do, and finishing it. Only then are you able to move forward, onward, and upward to embrace the next opportunity that is beckoning you.

When I was a boy scout, I was always inspired and motivated to reach the next level or rank. I couldn't wait to get my Tenderfoot Badge, and once I attained it, I applied myself diligently to rising through the levels of Second Class, First Class, Star and Life Scout, all the time inspired by this boy scout song:

Trail the Eagle

Trail the Eagle,
Trail the Eagle,
Climbing all the time.
First the Star and then the Life,
Will on your bosom shine.

Keep climbing!
Blaze the trail and we will follow,
Hark the Eagle's call;
On, brothers, on until we're Eagles all.[2]

Young scouts singing this song during their early years in scouting, then seeing the older scouts wearing their Eagle Badges, were motivated to work for this high honor. This was true in my own case. Upon achieving Eagle, I went on to become a Junior Assistant Scoutmaster before I eventually moved on from scouting into other high school and college activities. I may not have always been faithful to the principles and ideals of the Boy Scouts, but they gave me a foundation to build upon and to which I have always returned.

The Scout Oath

On my honor I will do my best
To do my duty to God and my country
    and to obey the Scout Law;
To help other people at all times;
To keep myself physically strong,
    mentally awake, and morally straight.[3]

Could any one of us aspire to anything less? And that is only the beginning. There is also The Scout Law which states, "A

---

[2]"Trail the Eagle," copyright © Edwin H. Morris Music Co. Inc. and Broadcast Music, Inc., NY; *Boy Scout Song Book* (Irving, TX: Boy Scouts of America).
[3]*The Boy Scout Handbook* (Irving, TX; Boy Scouts of America, 1990), p. 5.

scout is: trustworthy, loyal, helpful, friendly, courteous, kind, obedient, cheerful, thrifty, brave, clean, reverent."[4]

These principles set standards of excellence that provide a vital dynamic for consistent growth and progress. The Girl Scouts and Campfire Girls are based upon the same ideals. I have never met anyone who was part of these organizations in his or her formative years who was not grateful for them. Whenever I stray away from the teachings of the Boy Scouts (whose teachings are based upon Christianity and the universal spiritual principles in other religions), I become acutely uncomfortable.

For instance, I smoked for a number of years, but I always felt guilty whenever I lit a cigarette. I knew that I was breaking The Scout Law. I felt that I had broken a sacred trust. Eventually, I had the strength and good sense to cut it out.

I had never smoked in front of my father and mother, because I felt that I would be betraying their trust in me. Now I no longer needed to hide it. And on the physical level, I no longer needed to constantly clear my throat so that my voice would be clear for my work as an actor, teacher, and minister. When I was a boy, we jokingly called cigarettes "coffin nails," without actually realizing what truth we were speaking. Over the years, many of my friends and colleagues brought on their early demise by heavy smoking, which caused lung cancer— Gary Cooper, Robert Taylor, Carl Betz, Dick Powell, Humphrey Bogart, Robert Preston, and Yul Brynner, to mention just a few. What a waste!

Shortly before his death, wan, wasted, aged, and emaciated from the lung cancer that was ravaging his body, but still managing to perform the role of the king in the road tour of *The King and I,* Yul Brynner appeared in a series of TV commercials sponsored by the American Cancer Society. In a

---

[4]Ibid., pp. 7–8.

raspy, hoarse, weak, shaking voice he admonished, "Don't smoke. Don't smoke."

He didn't need to say anything else. His appearance told the rest. Yul died shortly after taping this public service announcement.

I stopped drinking alcohol for the same reason that I stopped smoking—it was no longer something I could allow myself to do, if I was to be true to my self-concept and the spiritual principles in which I believed and to which I had dedicated my life.

In spite of being brought up in a highly moral, deeply spiritual, teetotal home, and in spite of the Boy Scout Law and the teachings of Christianity, I tasted alcohol in my late teens, and sporadically through the years that followed. Social drinking was the accepted thing in the circles of which I was a part. Everyone did it. I enjoyed it, and so I did it, even though I never felt completely right about it. This feeling had nothing to do with morality. I just felt I shouldn't do it.

Finally, even though it had never been a problem, I eliminated alcohol completely from my life, because it was not compatible with my self-concept. I felt I could go further forward, onward, and upward without it. If you feel the same as I do, you will make the same decision I did. If you don't, you may find that the consumption of alcohol in moderation is acceptable to you. It may even have certain therapeutic benefits. However, if it is impairing your health or interfering with your work, or if you have become addicted to it, eliminate it completely from your life and never touch it again.

If the habit is too strong to allow you to go "cold turkey," seek help from Alcoholics Anonymous or other well-known treatment facilities that are available. The decision is up to you. The bottom line is that you must have control of your own life. If you can't drink, don't drink. It is as simple as that.

There is no middle path whatsoever in any hallucinogenic or mind-altering drug use. It is illegal, first of all, and the use of drugs of any kind is more destructive and even more of a world problem than most people are aware of. It is far too vast a subject to go into here. There has been much published about drugs, and there is a huge effort to deal with the problem by preventing and eliminating the use of them. The use of drugs for any reason other than medical use under strict supervision, is not an option for anyone; so don't even think about it. There is no question that the use of tobacco, alcohol, and drugs—raw stuff or pills—keeps you from moving forward, onward, and upward.

My purpose in life is to keep "trailing the Eagle" until I reach my full potential, and to help other people do the same. I say this, not to call attention to myself or my work, but to express the very strong conviction that this should be the life purpose for every one of us in the five and one-half billion-member human family. What other purpose could there be? What other option is there, except to "move better up to best"? The Psalmist sings, "I will lift up mine eyes unto the hills, from whence cometh my help" (Psalms 121:1). Isaiah gives us tremendous assurance that there is great strength and power available to us when we do our part:

> Hast thou not known? hast thou not heard, that the everlasting God, the Lord, the Creator of the ends of the earth, fainteth not, neither is weary? there is no searching of his understanding. He giveth power to the faint; and to them that have no might he increaseth strength.

> Even the youths shall faint and be weary, and the young men shall utterly fail:

> But they that wait upon the Lord shall renew their strength; they shall mount up with wings as eagles; they shall run, and not be weary; and they shall walk, and not faint. (Isaiah 40:28–31)

The intent of this book is to show you how to move forward, onward and upward to the attainment of your full potential, and the great rewards that come from devoting your life to this purpose. Paul tells of some of the qualities you will attain in moving toward your highest potential: "The fruit of the Spirit is love, joy, peace, longsuffering, gentleness, goodness, faith, meekness, temperance: against such there is no law" (Galatians 5:22, 23).

When you move steadily forward, onward and upward, you will be one with spirit, attaining your full potential. You will develop qualities and characteristics that give you dominion over your own life. Remember: you are not just a human being trying to make it through this world—you are a spiritual being going through a human experience on the way toward complete and perfect unfoldment of your real self. This is your spiritual self, and when you are expressing it, the "fruit of the Spirit" is yours. We will all reach the summit of the mountain some day, but in order to do that, we must constantly set our sights on it.

In order to view the full scope of your constantly beckoning new horizons, you must make the most of yourself on each one of the seven levels of the self—universal, spiritual, personal, mental, emotional, physical, and material.

UNIVERSAL HORIZONS

As you stay upon your trajectory, moving ever forward, onward, and upward, you are moving inward in the exploration of inner space. You must realize that all of your growth is the result of your awareness and perception of universal factors present within your personal individual self. The more the individual is universalized, the more the Universal is individualized. In other words, the more you identify yourself with God, the more Godlike you become.

O Lord our Lord, how excellent is thy name in all
the earth! who hast set thy glory above the heavens.

When I consider thy heavens, the work of thy fin-
gers, the moon and the stars, which thou hast ordained;

What is man, that thou art mindful of him? and the
son of man, that thou visitest him?

For thou has made him a little lower than the angels,
and has crowned him with glory and honour.
(Psalms 8:1, 3–5)

Since you are made in the image and after the likeness of
God in the first place, the attaining of your true spiritual identity is the discovery of what has always been there. It is the
return home. It is the seeking and finding of the kingdom of
heaven (universal beingness) within yourself. Contrary to
some religious teachings, there is no Heaven that we go to
some day to languish on pink clouds and slide down marble
balustrades throughout eternity, with angels as our constant
companions. No! Heaven is here right now, the state of perfect consciousness that can be attained when you apply yourself to developing the full potential of your universal self, your
awareness of God within you. It is attained through your consciousness of the presence of God, everywhere and at all
times. The secret of the mystery of forever moving toward
new horizons is that it goes on throughout eternity.

Since God is infinite, there can never be a boundary that
circumscribes Him. When you reach the horizon that once
beckoned you from such a great distance, you find that a new
one beckons you from an equally great distance; you move
forward, onward, and upward toward it. The process repeats
itself endlessly. It isn't so much that you reach one horizon
after another throughout eternity; there just appear to be dif-

ferent ones. But there is really only one horizon. You are constantly absorbing it and it is absorbing you. This is the meaning of omnipresence.

SPIRITUAL HORIZONS

On the universal level you are one with God, with no individual identity. The individualization process begins on the spiritual level, as God individualizes Himself as the Christ, the Son of God.

Every one of us is an "only begotten son of God" in that the "only begotten"—the Christ—is the real self of every one of us. Christ is not a person. The Christ is the individualization of Father-Mother God—the universal parent of all life, divine presence, universal principle. "Jesus" is a person, just as you and I are persons. Jesus Christ is the state of consciousness where the human and the divine are one. This is why you are a "spiritual" being, rather than just a "human" being. Your "humaness" does not start until you begin to function on the personal, or soul, level, which we will explore shortly. But first, continue to expand your spiritual horizons by recognizing four levels of Christ consciousness: Jesus, Jesus Christ, Christ Jesus, and Christ.

Jesus: Jesus is a man, but He is more than man. He is ultimate man, ideal man, perfect man. Think of Him as the great example, rather than the great exception. Jesus is your role model, the matrix upon which to pattern yourself. Strive to be like He is. Jesus is the apex of human evolution, where the human and the divine are one, completely unified and inseparable, indistinguishable from each other. Jesus is ideal man—the unification of the historical, the legendary, the mythological, the symbolic, and the mystical aspects of your being. Jesus is the symbol of what every person is and can become. "Jesus" is the first step in the four-level progression whereby the perfect man becomes the Son of God he was created to be.

Jesus Christ: This is the level of consciousness where the perfect human man (Jesus) is in balanced relationship with the Christ (spiritual man). As "Jesus Christ" you become aware that your exemplary human self is in complete partnership with the perfect divine self (Christ). That point where man and God conjunct, which we call "Jesus Christ," is an ancient concept, taught in the spiritual teachings of the ages, with many different names given to the components. Its meaning precedes Christianity, and transcends the literal teachings of orthodox Christianity, which limit and miss the point of the true spiritual teaching.

As you move forward, onward, and upward, you follow the path of Jesus, who became the Christ: "The child grew, and waxed strong in spirit, filled with wisdom: and the grace of God was upon him" (Luke 2:40).

Christ Jesus: Paul instructed, "Let this mind be in you, which was also in Christ Jesus" (Philippians 2:5). On this level, the spiritual man (Christ) rises above the human man (Jesus). The Crucifixion takes place on the Jesus Christ level when human limitation is crossed out of your consciousness and the vertical transcendence of the Christ is established. The Resurrection takes place on the third level—the Christ Jesus level.

You continue to live on the human level, but your true being is revealed as spiritual—as the Christ. At this point, Paul says, "I live, yet not I, but Christ liveth in me" (Galatians 2:20). As the Scripture states, ". . . the former things are passed away. . . . Behold, I make all things new" (Revelation 21:4, 5). The Ascension takes place as you ascend to the level from which you descended in the beginning.

Christ: Christ is the highest level of individual consciousness, the ultimate attainment, the final horizon. There is no higher individual or personal experience than Christ. "Christ in you, the hope of glory" (Colossians 1:27). Paul said, "I can do all things through Christ which strengtheneth me" (Philippians

4:13). The Christ is the Pearl of Great Price. With Christ you are everything; without Christ you are nothing. Christ ("I") is "the Way, the Truth and the Life." In Christ you are aware of your oneness with God. "No man cometh unto the Father, but by me" (John 14:6); "No man can come to me, except the Father which hath sent me draw him" (John 6:44).

All individualized identity begins and ends in Christ. The Christ is the essence that permeates your being as you move forward, onward, and upward toward the other levels of your personal eternal life experience.

PERSONAL (SOUL) HORIZONS

God is individualized as the Christ, and is personalized in the soul of each and every one of us. Your soul is what you are. Your soul is what God created out of Himself. "And the Lord formed man of the dust of the ground, and breathed into his nostrils the breath of life; and man became a living soul" (Genesis 2:7).

There are countless numbers of souls, each one absolutely unique. Your soul is your essence. Your soul is God expressing Himself through you at the level of your conditioned consciousness. Your soul is the vehicle that embodies the Christ, the perfect Son of God, the individuality of all living things. The soul is created in the "image and likeness" of God, and is therefore perfect in origin, but must become aware of its perfection and attain it through experience. Your soul lives forever and experiences many "lifetimes" or spans of experience under many conditions and circumstances, until, over a vast period of time, it regains its original perfection and returns to complete oneness with the oversoul—God—the one self.

In other words, the destiny of the soul is to move from "self-identity" to "Self-Identity." "Man does not live by bread alone, but by every word that proceedeth out of the mouth of God" (Matthew 4:4). "For what is a man profited, if he shall gain the whole world and lose his own soul?" (Matthew

16:26). These instructions seem to indicate that the real business of life is to develop your own soul by learning from the outer experiences of human existence, and by the inner experience of contact with God through identification with the Christ—to live, to love, to learn, and to serve—to move ever forward, onward, and upward.

MENTAL HORIZONS

Your mind is your most valuable tool. "Be ye transformed by the renewing of your mind" (Romans 12:2). It is at the medial area between your higher self (Soul, Christ, God) and your lower self (conditioning, body, experience). Your mind can go either way. Through it you have the power of choice. Of course, your mind will fluctuate between the concerns and needs of your human (lower) nature, and your spiritual (higher) reality. Both are important. The difficulty comes when you utilize your mind for human, worldly concerns and neglect to focus it upon spiritual factors. The ideal, of course, is to deal with both concurrently, because in the final analysis, everything is spiritual:

> Spirit as Spirit is Spirit.
> Spirit as Soul is Consciousness.
> Spirit as Mind is Intelligence.
> Spirit as Heart is Love.
> Spirit as Form is Body.
> Spirit as Activity is Experience.
> Spirit as Substance is Manifestation.

We must discipline the mind to discriminate between the important and the unimportant, between the necessary and the unnecessary, between the temporal and the eternal, between the earthly and the spiritual, between the real and the unreal, between appearance and truth, between human and divine. Your mind has a choice. What you choose determines what experiences you are going to have, thereby determining how much your mind is contributing to the advancement of your soul, onward and upward toward perfection.

Your consciousness determines your experience. And your consciousness can be changed through the use of disciplined techniques, which can build into your consciousness whatever quality you wish. You can see how important it is for you to understand how your thoughts change your life, and how necessary it is for you to keep moving forward, onward, and upward.

EMOTIONAL HORIZONS

Your feeling nature accounts for your aliveness and uniqueness as an individual entity. Consciousness (what you are) is the reality of your being, the distillate of what you think, what you feel, your spiritual awareness, and your experiential conditioning. Therefore, you see how important your emotional nature is in your total makeup. It is from your emotional nature that sensitivity and zest give flavor and color to your life.

Your emotional nature is the major component of your personality. When your feelings are predominantly negative, you obviously develop a negative personality. Negative emotions and feelings are the result of an overbalanced contact with and reaction to the false appearances and experiences of the world. In order to move forward, onward, and upward toward expanded emotional horizons, it is necessary to develop emotional qualities that are essentially spiritual.

Heart, in the Bible, is the name given the feeling (emotional) nature of man, and is sometimes extended to mean the entire subconscious mind. Your emotional nature is the head of steam—the powerhouse within you. It is your feelings that make everything happen—emotion, motion, motive, locomotive, automotive (self-activated). Your emotions must be balanced and controlled, otherwise they will run away with you.

Your mind must be taught to control your emotions, just as it must be receptive to the influence of your soul, which in turn is the expression of the spirit through the guidance of the Christ within. The mature individual is one who has balanced integration of all the seven levels of his being, including complete control of the emotions.

PHYSICAL HORIZONS

Your body is made to last as long as you have need of it—which is as long as you continue to grow and unfold and to do constructive and creative work during your earthly lifetime. Your physical body is needed in order to make possible your human experience. Your body is the vehicle that carries your soul during this human span of spiritual development. Your physical body is formed out of the substance of spirit, as blood, flesh, fiber, and bones. It is animated by spirit as the life force that manifests through you as structure, form, and function. Your entire physical organism is a highly organized and attuned instrument. The glandular and nervous systems integrate and unify the functions of the various internal organs that operate your circulatory, respiratory, digestive, heating, and cooling systems.

In addition to all these complex mechanisms are the five senses of sight, hearing, taste, touch, and smell, which provide the brain with information necessary for regulating, maintaining, sustaining, activating, and protecting the body. The brain, or cerebral cortex, is the head of the central nervous system, that vast network of nerves and ganglia that carries messages to every cell of the body.

The brain is the organ of thought, knowing, reasoning, learning, memory, conditioning, awareness, vision, perception, insight, understanding, wisdom, intuition, inspiration, and the building of consciousness. All of these aspects of consciousness act upon the body. The body cannot act of itself; it is acted upon. Every nuance of thought, feeling, and awareness has an effect upon the body. Your body is your consciousness in form and function.

Therefore, a constructive consciousness is the moving forward, upward, and onward toward new and higher physical horizons. Again, a sound mind in a sound body is the key. Your mind controls your body; therefore your thoughts and feelings must be positive, true, and pure. False beliefs and negative thoughts and emotions attack the body and cause illness and disease. The care of the body starts in the mind.

In addition to the control of consciousness as a basic requirement for physical health, so is the proper care of the body itself. This includes disciplined diet, rest, exercise, cleansing, and grooming. Temperance and regularity are essential in establishing and maintaining perfect circulation, perfect assimilation, and perfect elimination. The science of nutrition has made great advances in establishing new horizons for physical health. Regular exercise, ample rest, and meticulous personal hygiene are equally important. Take care of your body, and your body will take care of you.

MATERIAL HORIZONS

The seventh level is the most external area of your being. It includes everything in your environment—all the things you use, own, or are in contact with. We live in a spiritual universe, but our world is one of form and dimension, and includes many manifestations. The secret is to avail yourself of whatever it is you need, without becoming ensnared by objects, things, appurtenances, trivia, effluvia, and details. It is fitting, necessary, and proper to own things, but it is fatal to let them own you. "A man's life consisteth not in the abundance of the things which he possesseth" (Luke 12:15).

The first thing you must free yourself from is false belief in the desirability of accumulation. The material things of the world, including money, are to be used, not stored up to become burdensome and depleting impedimenta.

Lay not up for yourselves treasures upon earth, where moth and rust doth corrupt, and where thieves break through and steal:

But lay up for yourselves treasures in heaven, where neither moth nor rust doth corrupt, and where thieves do not break through nor steal:

For where your treasure is, there will your heart be also. (Matthew 6:19–21)

Actually, your possessions are an extension of your outer body. Have you ever said, when you were loathe to part with something, "Why, I couldn't do without that! It's part of me"? It seems that way because all the things you possess come to you out of your own consciousness; but they are not really part of you, and they have no power over you unless you give them that power.

Enjoy the material appurtenances of life. Eat good food, wear fine clothes, live in a comfortable, well-furnished home, drive a handsome, serviceable automobile; but do not make these things the focal point of your life. Keep in mind this principle: The higher mode of consciousness always governs the lower. For a fully developed, healthy self, the line of governing descent—universal, spiritual, personal (soul), mental, emotional, physical, and then material—shouldn't and really cannot be ignored.

Choose what you want in your life; bring it into your experience, and then release it as you continue forward, onward, and upward toward new horizons.

PERSONAL REALIZATION

New horizons are in view for me today as I move inward, forward, onward, and upward toward the fulfillment of my true potential.

My vision extends beyond that which I see. My insight is more penetrating than my thought. My awareness is higher than my thought. My understanding is greater than what I know. My love is unconditional and all-encompassing. My consciousness embraces the wholeness of total being.

The infinite expanse of the Universe fills my being today. I am one with That which extends beyond the One. I am an ongoing, ever-expanding activity of Truth. I am an Eternal Being, filled with the awareness and experience of Perfect Life. I see everything from the perspective of all and forever. I am not limited in any way. I function on a more lofty plane. I sing a new song; I sound a purer note on a higher octave. I draw a more beautiful picture. I generate a brighter light. I speak a more powerful word. I give a greater gift. I create a better world.

As I move toward the new horizons that beckon me, I release myself into the rhythmic, creative flow of Pure Spirit. I am Spiritual Being. I am an integral microcosm with God, the Macrocosm. I drink deeply from the wellsprings of Everlasting Life. I am joyously alive, alert, and attuned. My soul reflects the Perfect Christ of my Higher Self. My soul is aligned with the Divine Presence, and the Essence of God fills my soul with Itself. I am filled with awe and reverence as I am still and know my oneness with the One.

My individual consciousness emerges from the high awareness that fills my mind with noble thoughts and my heart with loving feelings. My love is unconditional. I love God; I love Life; I love myself. I love other people; I love the creative thrust of Spirit that moves me ever forward, onward, and upward to new and more glorious horizons. In the Name and through the Living Power of the Christ of Father-Mother God.

CHAPTER 8

GIVE YOURSELF AWAY

Mary Kay Ash, the founder of Mary Kay Cosmetics in Dallas, Texas, is as well-known for her charitable giving to worthy causes as she is for her fabulous business success. She gives out two golden shovels, fastened together—one small one, which we give with, and one large, which God gives with. Her observation is, "You can't outgive God."

Mary Kay tries, and she inspires others to try also. The net result is that, even though we can't outgive God, we can certainly outgive ourselves—outgive the level of our previous giving, no matter how much we have given.

The Scripture says, "Freely ye have received, freely give" (Matthew 10:8). We have been given so much. God has given us life, and our magnificent spiritual, mental, emotional, and physical equipment to live it with. All of our needs are provided for: "It is your Father's good pleasure to give you the kingdom" (Luke 12:32).

God is the source of our supply, and we will never lack for any good thing. Why then, do need, lack, suffering, deprivation, and starvation exist in our world? Largely because people operate on the "getting," rather than the "giving," principle and always have. This selfishness inevitably leads to oppression, conquest, and unequal distribution of life-sustaining resources, which give rise to suffering, starvation, and eventually war.

Just as the cycle constantly repeats itself in human history, so each one of us must go through unhappiness, insecurity, frustration, suffering, failure, and lack, until we reverse our thinking and learn how to give, rather than just to get. Those who learn to give instead of get find they now receive more than they did when their interest, attention, and effort were just concentrated upon themselves. There is a reason for this: giving is the universal principle that initiates and sustains the Law of Circulation. The Scripture instructs: "Give, and it shall be given unto you; good measure, pressed down, and shaken together, and running over"(Luke 6:38). Giving makes it possible to receive. Without giving there is no receiving. The cycle must be completed.

THE LAW OF CIRCULATION

In the Holy Land, there are two seas — the Sea of Galilee and the Dead Sea. The Sea of Galilee has both an inlet and an outlet. The water that circulates through it is fresh and sweet, and marine life, both flora and fauna, abound in its depths. The Sea of Galilee is fertile and productive, and just by giving of the fruits of its being, it supports the entire surrounding land and the multitudes who rely upon it for nourishment and refreshment. The Sea of Galilee is alive, and it gives life. The water of life circulates through it and flows on into the Dead Sea, which is in direct contrast to the Sea of Galilee.

There is no life whatsoever in the Dead Sea. The water is brackish and dead. The Dead Sea is stagnant because, even though it has an inlet that receives the fresh water of the River Jordan (the River of Life), which flows through the Sea of Galilee, the Dead Sea has no outlet. It only receives; it does not give. Therefore, it cannot live, and nothing can live in it. The surrounding desert land is sterile and lifeless, as is the entire area.

So it is with the individual who receives but fails to give. It is the giving that causes the circulation; it is circulation that gives health, increased abundance, and prosperity on every level. Giving is a way of life.

People fall into two categories: givers and takers. Be a giver, and you will never lack for any good thing. Be a taker, and even though you may attain temporary gain and advantage, your entire life will be a struggle. There is no middle ground. Decide right now to be a giver, and your life will change dramatically. Go all the way with life, and life will go all the way with you.

This approach to life will help you understand what Jesus was talking about when He said, "I am come that they might have life, and that they might have it more abundantly" (John 10:10). He was not talking about Himself as a person. He was talking about the way of life that is based upon the inner "I" — the consciousness of gratitude, graciousness, compassion, love, and givingness. Go all the way with this principle: give everything to life, and life will give everything to you.

Actually, God gives everything to us first, by giving us life. We have freedom of choice whether we comply with our giving part of the bargain or not. When we do learn to give, we find that a balance is established and maintained on every level of our lives. This is the Secret of the Ages.

THE PRINCIPLE OF TOTAL COMMITMENT

When Jesus instructs, "Go and sell that thou hast, and give to the poor . . . and come and follow me" (Matthew 19:21), He is not commanding us to indiscriminately give away everything we have to the poor in order to follow Him. In fact, He is not saying that we should follow Him as a man at all. He is telling us to give up all "poor" things, and follow the principle of total commitment by giving ourselves, our efforts, and our substance for the good of all — to the "poor," who are not as rich in understanding as we are when we learn to give.

He further instructs, "Whosoever [an idea, a principle] . . . shall compel thee to go a mile, go with him twain [all the way]" (Matthew 5:41). In other words, go all the way with what you know to be true.

We all know that "it is more blessed to give than to receive" (Acts 20:35), and that "God loveth a cheerful giver" (II Corinthians 9:7). Why then do we hold on to the old ways of getting, taking, accumulating, and withholding? If we withhold from life, life withholds from us. Giving and receiving are part of the same action. You cannot give without receiving. You cannot receive without giving; but all too often we fail to complete our part of the bargain, with disastrous results to ourselves. When you fail to give, you are actually stealing from yourself. When you compromise with giving, it constricts and limits your consciousness, thereby restricting the supply of good that is waiting to manifest in your experience.

Giving and receiving have to do with all areas of your life, not just money and other tangible, material goods. Giving has to do with everything. It has to do with material (monetary) prosperity, of course, but in a larger sense it has to do with your health, your happiness, and overall well-being. In this sense it is in your own best self-interest to give. Once we realize that the more we give the more we receive, how can we keep from giving all that we have and all that we are?

My personal realization of this principle has been the greatest discovery of my life. I had no knowledge of it whatsoever while I was growing up during the Depression, or even into my early adult years. I thought only of myself and how I could get ahead. I had a good religious upbringing, but I had no idea what the Bible teachings about giving and receiving meant, or how they applied to me. I thought they were nonsense. "Give all that you have to the poor. . . ." Really! I needed everything I could get for my own use. I wasn't as loving, kind, helpful, and understanding to others as I could have been, either. I was entirely self-centered. I always thought of myself first. I didn't know anything about the law of giving and receiving, and if I had known, I wouldn't have seen how it applied to me.

It is my observation that this is still pretty much the case with most of us, and accounts for many of the problems and difficulties still rampant in the world today, thousands of years after this great principle was first taught. Solomon taught it, Moses taught it, the Old Testament Prophets taught it, Jesus taught it, Paul taught it; and it is widely taught today in all religious and spiritual approaches, but the principle of "as you give, so shall you receive" is largely ignored. As Emerson pointedly asked, "In all of Christendom, where is the Christian?"[1]

Among all of us who are abundantly receiving all of the time, how many are givers? I was recently listening to a wonderful cultural program on the local community National Educational Television station, when the program was interrupted by a plea for funds. During the appeal, the manager of the station made the startling statement that less than 10 percent of those who enjoy the NET telecasts contribute to the support of the station, whose sole support comes from contributions from the viewing audience. The announcer exclaimed, "How can this be! It isn't fair! If you are enjoying these programs, shouldn't you give toward their support? Please send in your contribution now!"

And he went on to beg for funds from the 90 percent who were taking but not giving. Unbelievable, but not an unusual situation among public television stations, which are often the most popular in the community.

As a minister, I am not unfamiliar with human lethargy and diffidence when it comes to giving! However, the giving record in New Thought churches is usually much higher than

---

[1] R. W. Emerson, "Self Reliance" in *Emerson's Essays* (London: Arthur L. Humphreys, 1899), p. 93.

in many of the older orthodox churches. This is undoubtedly due to the fact that the laws of prosperity are taught, and people are encouraged to practice tithing.

THE LAW OF TITHING

Not all New Thought people practice tithing, of course, but an increasing number are doing so. *Tithe* means *one-tenth*. The ancient teaching in the Old Testament is that the "first fruits"—the first 10 percent of the harvest (the income)—belong to God. Therefore, this 10 percent is not ours in the first place. In the ancient agrarian society, 10 percent of the grain was set aside for planting the new crop. It was given back to the earth. One-tenth of the flocks were given to the glory of God in offered sacrifice and for building His temples and carrying on His mighty works.

As long as the people gave their tithe, they prospered. This is true in modern times as well. When people practice tithing—returning 10 percent of their income to God by giving their tithe to the church or spiritual organization through which they receive their spiritual sustenance—the individuals and the groups both prosper.

Tithing brings order into financial and personal affairs. I began to tithe many years ago and have prospered and been blessed in every area of my life ever since. "There has never been an ex-tither." Once you make it a regular practice to give the first 10 percent of your income to a spiritual organization, your life will change, and you will experience order in every area of your life.

Tithing is a commitment on your part to participate in the creative flow of the universe. God gives everything to us. Doesn't it seem reasonable that we return 10 percent to Him?

You may find it rather difficult at first. I did. You may say, "I can't afford to tithe." But after thinking about the principle involved, ask yourself, "Can I afford not to?"

Out of this process will come your decision to try tithing. It will be the greatest day of your life. Here is a suggestion: if giving 10 percent of your income is too abrupt for you, start with a lesser percentage — 5 percent, or even 3 percent. But be sure you make it a *proportionate* share of your income, given to God's work. The percentage principle is important. It must be high enough to be significant for you and to entail a real commitment on your part — something you want to do and are willing to undergo some sacrifice to fulfill.

Tithing is a way of life. It is a technique of ultimate giving that activates the flow of infinite abundance in your life, and in the activity of the spiritual organization you support. Tithing completes your circle of giving and receiving. Your fortunes are not left to chance. They are now governed by a scientific principle that never fails to reward those who initiate the law of circulation by giving.

Financial tithing of one's income is vital, but it is only one step toward total giving of yourself on every level. Start by tithing of your "time, talent and treasure," and you will progress to the level where you give yourself totally all of the time. That is what life is all about — giving.

Why else would God give us life? Why else does a flower bloom, other than to share its color and perfume? Why else does the bird sing, other than to lift our hearts in joy? Why else does the Sun shine, except to give us light, warmth, and life itself? Why else does the rain fall, other than to freshen the parched earth and to bring the thrust of life to all growing things? Why else does the air envelop and circulate around our planet, other than to nourish us by filling us with itself?

Everything in nature gives just by being itself. Except for humans, nothing else thinks of itself as separate in any way. The fish just is; the animal just is; the tree just is — everything just is — and in being, gives.

> Consider the lilies of the field, how they grow;
> They toil not, neither do they spin:

> And yet I say unto you,
> That even Solomon in all his glory
> Was not arrayed like one of these.
> (Matthew 6:28–29)

At a "thanksgiving" meeting at his church, one gentleman said, "Don't think you can ever give yourself away!"

Since he had just been admonished to "Give yourself away," it seemed contradictory. However, he quickly clarified his observation by explaining, "You can't give yourself away, because no matter how much you give, God has given you more to give. You can't give as much as there is, so give as much as you can, and everything will adjust itself."

This "giver" had discovered, on his own, Mary Kay's maxim, "You can't outgive God." Giving is love in action, and "love is the fulfilling of the Law" (Romans 13:10).

Tithing is a technique of giving that opens up the great possibilities of giving that life offers you. You become part of the life of everyone and everything when you give. The principle is to hold nothing back—to give whatever is needed, to whoever needs it, and at the time when it is needed.

There is one more consideration to make when giving. I call it the great secret of giving: Don't tell anyone about your benefices. Don't let the beneficiaries find out; if they should find out and thank you and feel beholden to you, it spoils the whole thing, and does not count. The mystical power of secret giving is dissipated, and its benefit is lost. Your giving is between you, yourself and God. Jesus explains this principle when He says:

> But when thou doest alms, let not thy left hand know what thy right hand doeth:
>
> That thine alms may be in secret: and thy Father which seeth in secret himself shall reward thee openly. (Matthew 6:3, 4)

Furthermore, Jesus gives us a very direct command: "Feed my sheep" (John 21:16); "inasmuch as ye have done it unto one of the least of these my brethren, ye have done it unto me" (Matthew 25:40). You may not be your brother's keeper, but you are certainly your brother's brother. Whatever you are, whatever you have, give it. Hold nothing back. You only have what you give away. You live that you may give; you give that you may live.

HELPING OTHERS

Equally as important as accomplishing what you set out to do is helping others accomplish what they want to do. This opens up a great avenue of giving for you. Listen to what your friends have to say. Take time to hear them out. Answer their questions; explain what you know; give them love and understanding; give them encouragement. Do not give too much advice, which is not really giving (it may be imposing your opinion and will upon others), but give freely of the knowledge and information you may have.

And be sure to give others the benefit of your experience and the lessons you have learned. All of this may take time, but remember, never miss an opportunity to put the Universe in your debt. Your giving to others may well start a chain reaction that continues with their giving, which then continues, ad infinitum. What you give today lasts throughout infinity, and is actually one phase of your own immortality.

When you help others, you are helping yourself. Giving builds self-esteem. You feel better about yourself when you help others. Giving provides you with a sense of purpose and personal significance. Giving lifts you out of any tendency toward discouragement and despondency. Giving brings your life into focus.

At one time, after I had been a minister for a number of years, I hit an empty period in my life and in my ministry. I was working hard, but with very little results. I felt that I was just going through the motions. I was feeling sorry for myself, much like Shakespeare's Hamlet when he lamented:

> How weary, stale, flat, and unprofitable,
> Seem to me all the uses of this world!
> Fie on it! ah fie![2]

In this maudlin state of self-pity, I went to see my mentor, Manly Palmer Hall, as I did so often in those days in the 1950s and '60s. He listened to my tale of woe with compassion and understanding as I told him how I felt.

"Are you helping anyone?" he asked, finally.

"Oh yes!" I replied. "I'm helping a lot of people. They depend upon me for help. After all, I am their minister. It's my job to help them."

"Exactly! It's your job to help them. It's not only your job, but it is your privilege, isn't it? Isn't that what you became a minister for in the first place? What right have you to get discouraged and feel sorry for yourself? No one put you in this position but you, yourself, did they?"

"No," I answered, chastened.

"And remember," the wise man continued, "if you help one person once in your lifetime, you have justified the reason for your existence."

"One time—only?" I faltered. My teacher had given me a whole new area of understanding. "Helped someone once in my entire life?"

"That's right!" Mr. Hall affirmed. "Now, be on your way and give people what you have to give them. They will be helped—and so will you."

I was inspired and joyously uplifted as I left my beloved teacher and hurried back to my ministerial tasks, thankful that as I performed them, I could help and give to others. Whenever the thrust of my giving wavers, I remember, "If you

---

[2]W. Shakespeare, *Hamlet*, Act I, scene 2, ll. 133–135.

help one person once during your lifetime, you justify your reason for existence."

Think of how much you have to give. When you give, you are helping, so your life has purpose and meaning. Give yourself away, and the riches of the kingdom are showered upon you.

At another time, after I had been teaching from the *Science of Mind* textbook, by Dr. Ernest Holmes, for fifteen years as a Religious Science minister, I again became bogged down and went to see Mr. Hall for counsel and guidance.

"What is it this time?" he queried.

"It's this book," I replied, as I held up the weighty *Science of Mind* textbook.

"What about it?" Mr. Hall asked. "What's wrong with it?"

"Nothing's wrong with it," I replied. "It's a great book. But enough is enough. I have been teaching from it for fifteen years in the Religious Science Accredited Classes, and I don't think I can do it another year. I don't think I have anything more to say about it."

"I'll tell you what," Mr. Hall mused, as he leafed through the several hundred pages of the Religious Science "bible," "this year, teach between the lines."

Wow! The impact of my mentor's instruction struck me with a direct hit. Of course, I realized, this year I'll teach between the lines. And I will have a lot more to give to my classes than I have ever given them before. Ernest Holmes gave to me through his textbook, Manly Hall gave to me through his counsel, and now I continue to give to my classes. Wow!

That's the way it worked out. As my consciousness was expanded by increased giving, my students received more, and I received more. I try always to continue following this sequence of giving. If I fail to do so, I soon find it out. Giving is a way of life, and all things proceed from the giving mind. We are here in this life to live, to learn, to love, and to give.

GIVING IS A WAY OF LIFE

There have been many men and women down through the years who have inspired me with their philosophy. In my first church there was a man who contributed regularly and generously. I made a point of thanking him each time he gave. His response was, "Don't thank me, Dr. Don. I ought to thank you for giving me the opportunity to give."

Giving was his way of life. Everybody gained by it. "The more I give, the more I have," he was fond of saying, "and the more I have the more I can give."

Our little church was struggling to make ends meet until this generous man showed us the secret of prosperity — giving. His generous contributions helped the church, of course, but of even more help was the prosperity consciousness he brought to everyone by his example. Others started to follow his lead. The church prospered, and so did they. One man caught the true spirit of giving when he said, "The money I give is not mine in the first place. It belongs to God. I just have the privilege of distributing it."

Giving is prosperity in action. Giving is both cause and effect. It is the cause of your prosperity, and it also is the effect of your prosperity, because the more you prosper, the more you want to give.

One lady who dedicates her life to giving generously of herself tithes of her "time, talent and treasure," but she sets her standard of tithing far above the traditional 10 percent of her income. She tithes not only on what she makes as income, but on what she *wants* to make. She makes her living through commission sales, and is always setting new goals and new quotas for herself. She is always aiming toward a higher target. She sets an actual figure of income much higher than what she is making now, and makes her tithe on this higher figure.

"I'm always doubling and tripling my income," she says. "It's very simple. By giving to God what belongs to Him, I make Him my partner. He never lets me down. We have a very good partnership."

Giving is the best possible way of giving thanks for your abundance. Along with the action of giving is the building of your prosperity consciousness by the continuous use of affirmations. Repeat the following statements until they are permanently entrenched in your subconscious.

God is the Source of my supply. The Infinite Law of Abundance flows through me. I am the channel of love and blessing through which all good things are expressed. I have more than enough to meet all of my requirements. I have a lavish and dependable income consistent with integrity and mutual benefits. The Father knows what things I have need of before I ask Him. All that the Father has is mine. It is the Father's good pleasure to give me the kingdom.

Be a prosperous person. A prosperous person is a giving person. A giving person is a prosperous person. We give that we may live. Give everything you have to make the world a better place in which to live. What other purpose could there be for living? Mother Teresa, "the Saint of Calcutta," in her great work of service to humanity, has said, "Service is not finding what you have to do, but in finding what fills you up, and doing that with all your heart." Everyone is inspired by this remarkable, loving, serving force for good on our planet.

Give your life in service to others, and you will not only bring untold benefits to them, but you will find personal fulfillment and benefits beyond anything you ever dreamed of for yourself. "Loving, self-forgetting service is the shortest, the safest, the surest road to God."[3]

Far from the usual concept of service as being sacrifice, this elevates giving through service to an entirely new and higher level. You do not lose, you gain through service. You

---

[3] A Rosicrucian adage.

do not suffer, you are exalted. You do not feel pain, you feel ecstasy. When you serve the Self, your self and the self of everyone else is served. Do what you do with all your heart and you will be inspired to direct your talents and efforts into myriad ways of serving others. There are opportunities for service on every hand, but you do not need to look for them. Just be yourself at your highest and best at all times, and do what you do to the best of your ability, and you will be serving in the highest possible way.

How to Give Effectively

We have indicated that the guideline for financial support for giving to your church or spiritual organization should be the tithe (10 percent of your gross income). Some people choose to compute their tithe on their net income, but the true tithe is on the gross. We must handle this in our own consciousness. We must also make our own decisions about giving to charity and charitable organizations or institutions. Technically, neither contributions to charity and worthy causes nor support given to family members or other needy individuals is counted as your tithe. The tithe is 10 percent of your income, given to God's work through the church or spiritual organization through which you receive your spiritual nourishment.

The need is great in many areas, and every loving, right-thinking person wants to give as much as he or she can. Obviously, we can't give to everything, and choosing what to give to is often difficult. There are some guidelines that will help. First of all, give because you want to—because you have decided it is the right thing to do. Don't give because you feel that you have to. This only leads to resentment and guilt should you fail to give. Token giving to quiet your conscience is not really giving.

Charitable giving is a science. Take time to study how and to whom you should give. It is possible that giving money, in certain instances, may do more harm than good.

The beggar may need food and clothing, but a handout may harm him by prolonging his dependence upon outside help rather than upon himself. "Don't just give a person a fish; teach him how to fish." This means that you must give yourself with your gift, by giving attention, instruction, inspiration, and encouragement.

We are all responsible for giving help to those in need. An immediate gift may temporarily help to meet a need, but it does not alleviate the cause of the lack. Therefore, one of your guidelines should be to give to organizations, funds, and research projects that are working to correct existing evils.

Finding out about how to give effectively is often the major part of the process of giving. Give yourself to your giving. Give until it feels good, and what you give will do good. In the final analysis, true giving is giving of yourself. You can't hold anything back. Whatever you are, that you must give, otherwise you will lose it.

> For unto every one that hath shall be given, and he shall have abundance:
>
> But from him that hath not shall be taken away, even that which he hath. (Matthew 25:29)

To him who has what? Love, understanding, generosity, compassion—the consciousness of God indwelling. "Freely ye have received; freely give" (Matthew 10:8). If you would have all, give all. If you do not give all, you will lose all.

Give your constructive consciousness for the benefit of others. Know good things for them. Encourage them. Inspire them. Love them. Bless them. Pray with and for them. God gives to all of us through the givingness of each of us.

Personal Realization

All the Universe is giving itself to me today. The multitudinous blessings of the Infinite are showered upon me. I am in the mainstream of Life. There is no place where God leaves off and I begin.

The Law of Circulation unites us in a never-ending continuum of giving and receiving. God gives to me. I receive from Him, and I give to Him. I give God my Life and my Love. I give Him all that I am and all that I have. I hold nothing back. I participate with God in the great process of Creation.

I give to Life and Life gives to me. I am interested in everything that is. I give my attention to the great works of the Spirit that are taking place within me and through me. I am enthusiastic about the processes of Nature. I give awe and wonder to the magnificence that surrounds me and beckons me to participate in the great drama of life and living. I give to Life and Life gives to me.

I give unconditional Love to all living and growing things. I behold the Divinity in every blade, bush, and flower. I give my awareness of the holiness of every creature that flies, swims, crawls, or walks. I give up my little self as I am immersed in the wonder and glory of all Being.

I give myself to my brothers and sisters of the human family. I seek to "heal the sick, cleanse the lepers, raise the dead, [and] cast out devils" (Matthew 10:8). I seek to help. The more I help, the more I give. The more I give, the more I live.

I give my strength to help the weak. I give my joy to lift the downhearted. I give my encouragement to those who are frustrated and discouraged. I give the Christ to those who are lost. I care about everyone.

The undulating tides of Life give sustenance and refreshment to me. I keep the channels of my consciousness open so that I may fully give now and forever. And so it is.

CHAPTER 9

BE HERE

We live in the here and the now. This is the only moment in eternity that we know anything about. The past is gone, and the future is yet to be; so, be here now. If anyone asks you what time it is, the answer is, "Now!"

This is the first moment of the rest of your life. Make the most of it. Cherish it. Love it. Appreciate it. Give thanks for it. Your entire life is determined by what you do with this moment, because the progression of moments forms the structure of eternity. You live forever, one moment at a time. As you make the most of each moment, you are building the substance of your life. You are determining the events and experiences that will come to you as your life unfolds. As Paul says, "Beloved, now are we the sons of God, and it doth not yet appear what we shall be" (I John 3:2).

Material science tells us there is limitless energy in a single atom; mental science shows that there is infinite potential in a single thought, a single feeling, a single moment. The nuances and vibrations of your thoughts and feelings release unlimited energies, which work creatively in every aspect of your life.

Spiritual science reveals that you live forever in the eternal unfoldment of time, which consists of continuous beingness. To completely participate in the here and the now, and to completely develop your sensitivity on every level, you must be: alive, alert, awake, aware, attuned, and active.

ALIVE

Affirm: *The free, full flow of life is surging through me, developing every level of my being and integrating every aspect of my consciousness.*

Above all things, you are a living being, participating in the great wonder and mystery of life. Jesus said, "I am come that they might have life, and that they might have it more abundantly" (John 10:10). Remember that spirit is life, and that you are a spiritual being living through a human experience on the way toward complete and perfect unfoldment of your real self. This can only be accomplished by living your life fully, every moment.

Even though they may be breathing and moving, many people are more dead than alive. Arise to the full life by developing your interest, sensitivity, and enthusiasm. Live your life fully in every way, all the time.

ALERT

Affirm: *I am eager and alert at all times. I am always ready for every opportunity that comes my way. My physical, mental, emotional, and spiritual antennae are always up—sensitive and receptive.*

Don't let life pass you by. Be alert to the messages that are constantly coming to you from within yourself and from the world around you. Be alert to what life is endeavoring to tell you. Sharpen your physical senses, and be alert to the data they are providing for you. See clearly. Hear clearly. Be alert to the input from your senses of touch, taste, and smell. Learn discrimination and good judgment by being alert to what is being presented to you through your physical and spiritual senses and your experiences as they help you become aware of the higher powers within you.

AWAKE

Affirm: *I am constantly awake, physically, emotionally, mentally, and spiritually. I am refreshed and renewed as I dissolve all lethargy, release all concerns, and spring forth with interest and enthusiasm.*

"Awake thou that sleepest" (Ephesians 5:14). Of course, sleep is important, but one should be wide awake when not sleeping. The best direction is to sleep when you sleep, but be fully awake the rest of the time. Life is for living fully, and we are only half living unless we are fully awake. To be awake is to fully participate in the celebration of life going on around you and within you. Awaken your instincts, your senses, your reflexes, your feelings, your thoughts, your entire consciousness, to experience the most and the best of life.

AWARE

Affirm: *I am aware of who I am, why I am here, and where I am going. I am aware of much more than meets the eye. I am sensitive to subtleties and nuances. I am aware.*

There are two kinds of people: those who know and those who do not. Those who don't know are simply not aware. They are not "with it." There are many messages and communications for the person who is perceptive and aligned with what is going on. Aware individuals are receptive to both sensory and extrasensory stimuli: they respond even more to the invisible than to the visible. They discern the unseen. They hear the unspoken. They are able to find the inner meaning. They sort out every detail of the hidden agenda. You are incomplete unless you are aware. Your awareness enables you to fill in the blank spaces.

ATTUNED

Affirm: *I am attuned to the vibrations around me. My heart is beating in rhythm with the heart of the universe. I sing the song of life. I vibrate to the celestial chords. I am in harmony with the divine melodies.*

Just as a tuning fork vibrates to the note that is struck on the piano, so each one of us vibrates to the notes that sound around us and within us. This principle is sometimes called the law of reflection, or the mirror principle. We reproduce in our consciousness the vibrations of both the outer and the inner. Do not react to the discordant notes of negativity and imperfection, but attune your instrument of perception so that you are always in harmony with the good, the true, and the beautiful. Paul is teaching the law of attunement in the following passage.

> Finally, brethren, whatsoever things are true, whatsoever things are honest, whatsoever things are just, whatsoever things are pure, whatsoever things are lovely, whatsoever things are of good report; if there be any virtue, and if there be any praise, think on these things. (Philippians 4:8)

ACTIVE

Affirm: *I am immersed in the activity of Life. I am a moving, creating, producing organism. I am an active part of the Life of the Universe. I live and move and have my being in the creative action of Life.*

All of life consists of the outer expression of inner states of consciousness. This is the creative process. The movement is always from within outward; the dynamic of the inner concept bursts forth in action and produces the outer manifestation. The subconscious of the individual is one with the universal subjective law, which receives the impress of our thought and acts upon it. Action follows thought.

In the creative process constantly taking place through us, there are three main steps: conception, gestation, and action. There is seed-time and harvest. There is no harvest without action. Think, then act!

How to Fully Be Here

The following affirmations to help us fully be here now are usually attributed to Emmet Fox:

> I have conscious Divine Intelligence.
> I individualize Omniscience.
> I have direct knowledge of Truth.
> I have perfect Intuition.
> I have spiritual Perception.
> I know.

Regular repetition of these statements will train your senses, thoughts, and feelings to be fully on duty at all times.

I have conscious divine intelligence. This affirmation makes you much more aware of the nature of your being. It expands the scope of your consciousness. It extends the realm of your self-concept. God is divine intelligence, and since you are made in the image, after the likeness of God, you are divine intelligence individualized. You have it, but you must *know* it.

The affirmation helps you know it, consciously. It gives you spiritual identity and lifts you into the acceptance of your unlimited potential. It helps you understand a statement Ernest Holmes made in a lecture: "The mind of man is marvelous. Every time he thinks, he sets the entire creative mechanism of the Universe into operation." Expand your awareness to accept the reality that you do have conscious divine intelligence.

I individualize omniscience. "Omniscience" is all-knowing. God is all and knows all. God, thinking within

Himself, upon Himself, about Himself, created the manifest universe. Whatever is true of God is true of you. It is just a matter of degree. God is the universal. You are the individual. God is omniscient, omnipotent, omnipresent, and omniactive. So are you, but you do not know it until you become consciously aware of it and believe it.

You already know everything there is to be known, and your eternal life is the process of developing the awareness, wisdom, and understanding that enables you to consciously confirm it. You must participate in the process of unfoldment. The attainment of your full development cannot be given to you. It must unfold *through* you. Start right now believing that you know everything there is to know, and that you are on the joyous journey of discovering and learning everything you already know.

I have direct knowledge of truth. "Ye shall know the truth, and the truth shall make you free" (John 8:32). What is this basic truth? The following lines succinctly and simply tell us:

> There is One Life.
> This Life is God.
> This Life is whole.
> This Life is perfect.
> This Life is my life now.

Affirming this helps it become true in your life, even though we all fall considerably short of demonstrating this truth. But the discrepancy between fact and the truth does not change the reality of the truth. Facts change; truth is constant. Truth transcends appearances and circumstances. Truth is your guiding star. Jesus, speaking as the Christ, teaches, "I am the way, the truth, and the life" (John 14:6). Develop Christlike qualities in every aspect of your life, and the truth will become fact. In the meantime, continue to affirm that you have direct knowledge of truth.

I have perfect intuition. Intuition is knowing without knowing how you know. It is the highest function of the individual mind; intuition is divine mind using individual mind. Intuition is not to be confused with instinct, which is the subconscious reflex of the autonomic nervous system — automatic response in line with the nature of our species. Our instincts are physiological and emotional; intuition is mental and spiritual. Both are important. You don't need to develop instincts; you just need to learn to discipline and control them. On the other hand, even though intuition is inherent within you, it needs to be developed and used so that it can guide you.

When your intuition speaks to you, listen to it and follow it. It is the "still small voice" that speaks when you become still and listen. In its most common appearance, we call it a hunch; in its highest expression, it is the direct influx of infinite intelligence from the mind of God.

I have spiritual perception. Paul says, "the natural man receiveth not the things of the Spirit of God: for they are foolishness unto him: neither can he know them, because they are spiritually discerned" (I Corinthians 2:14).

Unless you perceive things spiritually, you are seeing "through a glass darkly." Mental and emotional conclusions and reactions, and the testimony of the physical senses, may give us true perception part of the time, but they are unreliable. They often tell lies for various reasons: previous conditioning, false belief, prejudice, opinion, incomplete data, faulty interpretation of facts.

The reason there is so much error, disease, war, crime, starvation, and suffering in the world is that we believe our own lies. Our perceptions are factual, material, and physical rather than spiritual. We can change this only by following Jesus' admonition to "judge righteous judgment" (John 7:24).

"Righteous judgment" is spiritual perception. You have it. Learn to use it.

I know. This is the ultimate affirmation. It encompasses and includes everything else. To be—to live—is to know. What else is there? We are what we know. If we don't know much, we don't amount to much. Nothing comes from nothing. The tragedy is that even in the midst of our unknowing, we really *do* know, but don't *know* that we know. The "cloud of unknowing" hovers over us, not dissolving until we become aware and awake. In the meantime, this ancient proverb aptly applies:

> He who knows not and knows not
>   that he knows not,
> He is a fool. Avoid him.
>
> He who knows not and knows
>   that he knows not,
> He is simple. Teach him.
>
> He who knows and knows not
>   that he knows,
> He is asleep. Wake him.
>
> He who knows and knows
>   that he knows,
> He is wise. Follow him.[1]

Be a knower. You already *are*. Now, know that you know.

AREAS OF OMNIPRESENCE

In addition to the many areas of extended awareness we have been developing, the following seven are part of the anatomy of your mind and part of totally being here now.

---

[1]Ancient proverb. Used in D. Curtis, *Daily Power for Joyful Living* (North Hollywood, CA: Wilshire Book Co., 1974), p. 22.

Vision: The development of full awareness requires that even though you live in the here and now you learn to see beyond your sight. "Where there is no vision, the people perish" (Proverbs 29:18). True vision is that inner faculty that enables you to see beyond the visible. When Paul says that faith is the "evidence of things not seen" (Hebrews 11:1), and "[the] things which are seen were not made of things which do appear" (Hebrews 11:3), he was indicating that we have a level of perception that is much more real than the outer sense of sight, even though it does not deal in tangibles.

Vision is the faculty of inner seeing. Visualization is a form of vision on the psychological level; goal-setting is a use of vision on the mental level; clairvoyance is vision on the psychic level. But spiritual vision rises above all of these. Spiritual vision is the faculty of "seeing true." This faculty enables you to see the nature of things the way they really are, uninhibited by human limitation and interpretation. It enables you to perceive causes, rather than only effects.

Insight: This deals with the entire process of cerebration or brain action: thinking, reasoning, selecting, comparing, measuring, mulling, musing, observing, summarizing, concluding, correlating, synthesizing. Logic is essential to the intellect. Whether the thinking mind is reasoning inductively or deductively, what it deals with must be acceptable to it. It must make sense to you or you will reject it.

If you are to attain true insight, you must free your thought from the bondage of the "foolish consistency" that Emerson says is "the hobgoblin of little minds."[2] Insight is much more than just thinking. It is the original stuff out of which consciousness is built.

Imagination: This is the fountain from which comes thoughts, ideas, concepts, plans, and pictures of great worth

---

[2] R. W. Emerson, "Self Reliance" in *Emerson's Essays* (London: Arthur L. Humphreys, 1899).

and beauty. It is a superconscious spiritual faculty. There are no limits to your imagination except those placed upon it by your thought and conditioning. Great results can be achieved when your mind forms concepts and dares to imagine that they are true.

The imagination works both ways: as a receiver and means of gestation; as a channel and conductor for emanation from the infinite mind. In both instances the individual conscious mind is involved, but in the first instance it activates the imagination; in the second process, the imagination activates and stimulates the conscious mind, assisting it to rise above itself. In the first process, you are using your own mind and imagination to help you accept a desired good. In the second—higher—process, you are letting imagination itself, an aspect of the one mind, use your individual intelligence and imagination for purposes of spiritual unfoldment and expansion.

Imagination is not detachment from reality. It is reality itself. True imagination is not fantasizing or making things up. It is the medium through which you can accept the reality of infinite being and identify yourself with it. Nothing is too wonderful to happen; nothing is too good to be true.

Intuition: This is direct knowing. It is the process by which you can know something without the intellectual process of conscious thought. Intuition is an aspect of divine mind that functions in the individual mind, and can be developed as the highest of your mental functions, the activity of "Mind" that lifts you above the mind.

When the intuitive power is developed within you, you learn to rely more on God's reality than upon your own opinion and your own selection. When that still small voice of intuition speaks to you, listen to it. It is God, telling you what to do!

You have come to understand that man can know God, literally, and become one with God through his own mind.

Now that you understand it, do it. Go beyond thought. First you think clearly, then you know. This knowing is intuition.

> Inner knowing, quiet flowing
> Of the stream of life's pure being,
> Instructing, inspiring and uplifting me
> To higher levels of understanding and awareness.[3]

Perception: When you see anything in life as a threat or a difficulty, that is human perception. We tend to think of ourselves as human beings rather than spiritual beings; we think of ourselves as living in a material world. And therefore, we think the universe is material. We see it; we have five senses to help us interpret it; we form a concept and perceive things "out there."

Spiritual perception is human perception raised to a higher level. Move from your one-dimensional, sensory interpretation to the highest point of view. Now you can see that the problem, the challenge, the difficulty "out there" is really an opportunity—an opportunity to grow. Spiritual perception, spirit, the conscious mind of God, individualizes as the conscious mind of man, functioning as intelligence and thought. When you see things through your spiritual perception, the greatest possible good can be perceived, understood, and experienced. Consider the images and ideas in following poem:

> Upward and inward my mind flows
> Into the creative realm of my soul.
> I am released from the pressures of the world,
> I am free to rise to higher ground.
>
> Expanded horizons beckon to me
> To explore them, experience and express them.

---

[3]D. Curtis, "Voice of the Silence" in *Cosmic Awareness,* p. 31.

I am initiated into new perspectives
As I fly with the wings of Spirit.

My denser bodies fall from me
As I "leave my nets and follow Him"
Into the extended reaches of Being
And "dwell in the Secret Place of the Most High."

I have no plans to ever return to the
Mundane world of commonplace preoccupations.
My bonds are dissolved and I am free
To "dwell in the House of the Lord forever."

I am truly "transformed by the renewing of
    my mind,"
I am "lifted up with eagle's wings,"
"I may be weary but I will not faint,"
"I may stumble but I will never fall."

"And I, if I be lifted up from this earth,
"Draw all men unto me."
"I go to prepare a place for you,
"And if I go and prepare a place for you,
"I will come again and receive you unto myself,
"That where I am, there ye may be also."

The caterpillar of me has been metamorphosed
Into the butterfly of my True Self,
Which flies through eternity, beautiful and free,
An inspiration and a blessing to all.

Thank you, Father-Mother God.[4]

Understanding: This is how you use the sum total of all your mental processes. Understanding makes wisdom a living reality. Wisdom + Love = Understanding. An understanding

---

[4]D. Curtis, "Higher Ground" in *Cosmic Awareness,* p. 32.

person expresses both wisdom and love. These two together give you balance; balance and maturity. The wise person knows the laws of life—the understanding one knows how to use them.

The greater part of wisdom is in using it wisely. Understanding is knowing how to do so. Understanding could be described as knowing what to do, when, how, and where to do it. Understanding of yourself, of God, of the universe, of the world, and of the relationships between them helps you be more understanding of your fellow human beings who are on life's journey with you.

Inspiration: To inspire means to breathe in. Spirit is the breath of life; inspiration is the state and process of being filled with spirit. When you are inspired, you are literally filled with infinite intelligence and power.

Inspiration is that spiritual infusion which lifts you toward the expression of your full potential. When you are inspired, you rise above yourself. You are capable of thoughts, insights, expressions, and actions that you do not rise to at other times. Under inspiration, the artist becomes an instrument in the hand of the Creator; the composer tunes in on heavenly music; the speaker, the singer, the actor, the athlete all experience periods of inspiration when it is as if the words and ideas, the notes, the depth, and the movements all come from a level quite beyond their skill or comprehension, as if to shape them for the purposes and designs of a will above their own.

This, then, is inspiration: God flowing through man. You make yourself sensitive and susceptible to inspiration when you maintain order and harmony in your inner and outer life, and align yourself with all that is constructive. As you focus your mind upon the good, the true, and the beautiful, you become a transparency through which the light of the spirit shines and takes form in myriad ways as all that is good.

Truth

The immaculate essence of pure Truth
Enters in and fills my consciousness
With the substance of all wonderful things.

I am transformed by the renewing of my mind.
My soul is lifted up with eagle's wings,
I ascend to the summit of all experience.
I am monarch of all that I survey.

The transmuting vibrations of Spirit
Cleanse, purify and transfigure me.
I live eternally in the Light.[5]

Far from being "supernatural," you should think of inspiration as an inherent part of your true nature as a spiritual being. Is there anything more natural than to be filled with one's self? Since your self is the One Self—All That Is—inspiration is confirmation and expression of what you really are.

ACTIVITY OF BODY

Of spirit, soul, mind, and body, possibly the body is the most complex of all and probably the most important of all, because it is the most personal, the most immediate. It is your score card, your barometer. You read it first. And if you read something out of focus from your body—even signs of aging—that something needs to be corrected.

When we say "body," we instantly think of the physical body. But you have other bodies as well. As Paul said, "There is a natural body, and there is a spiritual body" (I Corinthians 15:44). "There are also celestial bodies and bodies terrestrial" (I Corinthians 15:40).

---

[5]D. Curtis, "Truth" in *Songs of the Soul*, p. 27.

The Spiritual Body: The health and wholeness of your physical body starts with the spirit, which is the mind of God, that power that knows itself. All things come from spirit. Spirit is light. Spirit is energy. Spirit, being the mind of God, must become manifest. So the manifest universe that we know is the body of God.

You are a native of eternity, a child of light, an inhabitant of the universe, and part of it. You are made up of the same stuff as the stellar galaxies. You are part of nature, part of all that is wonderful and good.

Knowing that about yourself becomes your first open doorway to health. When you think about your body, think first of all about your spiritual body, your light body, your energy body — your real self.

The Soul Body: The first point of individualization is the soul. God breathed into man the breath of life, and he became a living soul. Think of it this way: Your soul carries the spirit of God; your physical body, including the mind and the creative power of the subconscious, carries your soul, so they are linked together. You are threefold — spirit, soul (which includes mind), and body; the light body, which is spirit, and the soul body, which is the vibration of life energy within you.

The Mental Body: With the soul is the mental body. You've heard many times that thoughts are things, and you know it's true. You know that nothing really exists except when thinking makes it so. A thought held in mind produces after its kind. Actually, what you are is a spiritual, mental being walking through this earth experience, using a physical body, which is consciousness in form.

Be very careful as you create your own body out of your thoughts and your feelings. You have an emotional body, as you know from even a casual acquaintance with psychosomatic medicine ("psycho," *psyche*, which means *soul; soma*, which means *body*) — the soul-body relationship.

The Oracle at Delphi said: "The key to good health and to everything in life is, 'Man, Know Thyself.' " To know your real self, know there is light and life and love spirit within you. You know yourself by what you think about yourself.

BE WHOLE

Your body is a wonderful instrument. Your body is important; you are supposed to have it, and it has a very important function. Just for a moment, become aware of your body. Say to yourself: *I love my body! I know that this body is a wonderful, functioning servant.*

Your body has no way of knowing how to be a good master, but it does know how to be a good servant. It is completely receptive to your thoughts, feelings, and attitudes. Your body is made out of your attitudes, habits, thoughts, and feelings.

The actual substance of your body is the Universal Stuff of the different Kingdoms of Nature—Mineral, Vegetable, and, Animal. You are of homo sapiens, the Human Kingdom, but the material substances of all the other kingdoms exist in your body. For instance, you have minerals in the bony structure of your body. Your hair is vegetable; it grows, the same way that vegetables grow from the earth. Your senses, urges, desires are of the Animal Kingdom. The Kingdoms of Mineral, Vegetable, and Animal become Human within you.

If you are in tune with nature, the tendency is for you to be healthy, and to be healthy means to be made whole. To be made whole means to have a perfect, integrated balance among the spirit, the soul, the mind, the heart, the body, and your world of affairs.

In order to understand the body and to have perfect health, we need to retool our thinking. I've worked out a little doggerel:

Keep your mind clear,
Keep your heart warm;
Keep your body pure,
Keep your words kind;
Keep your actions controlled.

This body of yours is made to last—but it's up to you to determine for how long. We have different time cycles in our lives. You have been sent here on a field trip, and the world experience is the laboratory through which you grow. This soul of yours has lived forever, and it lives now, in a succeeding series of lifetimes. I don't know what you need to accomplish in this lifetime. I don't even know what I need to accomplish in this lifetime. But I do know that you can only accomplish it if you give all that you have, all the time.

When this cycle is over, I am sure it has been planned in the great scheme of things that the next step will be taken. But while you are here, you are supposed to take care of this body, even though to a large degree, it is capable of taking care of itself.

You have probably experienced healing in your body, whether you know it or not. Autopsies have revealed lesions and scars from great spontaneous healings that have taken place without any knowledge of any disorder. Your body has a great tendency—just as the universe—to always work toward perfection, to always return to *stasis,* which means a state of balance, of well-being. All it requires is that you pay some particular attention to it.

But in the world today, most people neglect their bodies—eating junk food and letting themselves become addicted to certain kinds of "stuff." You have been given a mind, which has choice. You can choose to do anything that you want. You can eat junk if you want to, you can get angry if you want to, you can think negative thoughts if you want to. (That's usually done by default, because you react to the things of the world, and the world moves in.)

I'm sure you have had a condition appear in your body that you could trace back to your own negativity or your own upset consciousness or, simply, to the fact that you just hadn't taken care of your body. Your body is like a child, and it loves to be taken care of. It loves attention. If you've been abusing it, it will call for that attention in no uncertain terms, in the only way it has to speak—through pain and indisposition.

One of Plato's teachings was that there is a perfect pattern of all things known in the Mind of the Infinite. If we get out of focus with that perfect pattern, disease sets in. It has been observed by scientists and philosophers down through the ages that when anything of a negative nature exists in the consciousness of the human race, it will be manifested in a disease.

From this background, let us see what you can do about the different illnesses that can come about in your body from time to time. For instance, let's look at something that has to do with the heart.

The heart is the headquarters of the circulatory system and is closely tied into it. The heart represents love; it represents the flow of life through your body through the bloodstream. Anything that interrupts the free, full flow of life through you—any kind of anxiety, hurt feelings, or pressure, is likely to affect your heart and bloodstream.

Don't let that frighten you—it does not mean that if you work under some pressure you are going to have heart or blood pressure problems. But the tendency is there. Whenever your thoughts become negative or destructive, or are completely swept into the confusion of the world, it will certainly affect the body.

The best kind of medicine is preventative medicine. Keep building your Golden Bridge each day; keep clear in your mind and warm in your heart. If you are challenged by things of the outer world, make peace with them rather than letting them get in and upset your body.

A lady who had unbelievably high blood pressure once came to me. She had tried everything, and had not been helped. Over a period of a few weeks—I saw her once a week—we affirmed: *The free, full flow of life is surging through me. There is calm, quiet, peaceful, silent, inner knowing.*

The blood pressure started to go down.

My heart is beating in rhythm with the heart of the Universe. I am in tune with the Stars and the Stellar Bodies. I am in tune with the natural cycles of Nature. I am whole. I am strong.

Within a period of about five weeks, her blood pressure was completely normal.

BLESS YOUR BODY

Your body is a very delicately attuned instrument. Look at the different systems that are operating in your body: the circulatory system, the nervous system, the digestive system, the respiratory system, and the cooling system, just to mention a few. These systems working within you are geared to a perfect inner pattern, but if you get out of focus with them—if there is too much hurry, worry, tension, pressure, anxiety—stress can result.

Stress is the number-one killer, because it gives rise to a whole body of other kinds of physical indispositions or disease (absence of ease). Your body has no choice but to react and express them.

So, bless your body. Visualize wholeness in it. Give thanks for it. Talk to your body. Love your body. Cleanse and purify your body. Also, and this is very important, take care in the adornment of your body. And then, make some personal choices.

Look at diet, rest, exercise, purification, and cleanliness. Pay particular attention to mental and emotional intake, and to the intake of food. The dietician would say, "You are what you eat," and to a very real degree, you are. Of course you are much more than what you eat, but what you eat is very important.

Start early. Start now. Eliminate the things you know are destructive from your diet. Intuitively, in the back of your mind, there is a little voice that warns, "No, that's not good." But perhaps you say, "Oh, just this once doesn't count."

"This once" becomes twice, and then it becomes multiplied. Geometric progressions set in, and after a while you're in trouble, all as a result of something you *could* have just stopped doing. There is something most wonderful about putting yourself in charge of your own life.

What you feel is very important, too. Do you have feelings of love? Of kindness? Do you have feelings of joy? Of peace? If you don't, make a change. Put your mind in control. If you see yourself acting negatively or destructively, learn to watch your thoughts, your feelings, and correct them.

This process is called denial and affirmation. Deny anything unlike the nature of God. Affirm: *The free, full flow of Life is taking place through me on every level.* You will find that this kind of preventative procedure enables you to establish yourself in a basic, healthful, holistic relationship to life.

Your body does not act by itself; it is acted *upon*. Whatever is done about your body has to come from somewhere else. That "somewhere else" is not in the outer; it is another level of your own consciousness. Even if medicine or doctors should come into the picture, the actual healing is not going to be done *to* you; it will be done *through* you.

Never—never—never—never—NEVER give up! Never, never feel that anything is incurable or any problem or difficulty is insoluble, because it is not. There are wonderful examples of people who, given the word that some incurable condition—usually cancer—was in their body, supposedly incurable, have experienced remission. They reversed their thought and are strong and vital and whole.

Many people who, a number of years ago, received a "death sentence," are now strong and vital. There was a recent newspaper story of a young man with the AIDS virus who was told that he had at the most six months to live. That's been a matter of over three years ago now. He has devoted his life to helping others to understand that positive thinking heals any condition. The headline reads: "Positive Thinking Heals AIDS Situation."

There are no exceptions. The principle is the same. "According to your faith be it unto you" (Matthew 9:29). "Thy faith hath made thee whole" (Mark 5:34).

I know something about hospitals—and operations—and negative thinking. Once, years ago, I came to one morning—or night—in the receiving ward of a New York hospital just in time to hear an intern say, "He won't last till morning."

I was 31 years old. I had just come from a career in Hollywood that went up like a skyrocket—and then fizzled and fell down. I was upset and disappointed, bitter and angry. Finally, inevitably, an old weakness of my body had taken over.

I was born with a congenital kidney malformation that malfunctioned whenever I was under emotional stress. I had always been able to live with the condition and weather pain attacks, but this time, aggravated by my negative feelings of anxiety and worry, the kidney stopped functioning and "blew up," making surgery necessary.

I called my minister, Raymond Charles Barker, at his New York home at about four o'clock in the morning. I could just gasp out, "I'm in the hospital!"

"You know how you got there?" he asked.

"Yes, I do," I mumbled.

"Then you know how to get out, don't you?" he said. And hung up!

I am glad that he did, because it put me on my own. I knew that if I was going to get out of the hospital, I was going to have to do it myself. Somehow or another I took hold and got through it.

With a sense of gratitude, I went back to my life. And I did just as I had done before. Soon I was back in the hospital again. I had trouble in another part of my body. Even though my kidney had been removed, it was only the symptom. The cause was my negative consciousness. I came out, still not cured, still not healed, but beginning to see the light. I began to use some of the things I had been studying.

The chronic condition in my body had been there since I was a child. I was able to trace it back to its psychosomatic origins: insecurity, trying too hard, feelings of inferiority, and guilt. I started to correct those feelings and used affirmations and healing prayer regularly. Finally, after a number of months — one morning it was over! The condition was no longer there. Complete normalcy had set in.

A few years ago, I could hardly open or close my hands. I couldn't grip a golf club, and I love to play golf. I sold my membership at the local golf club. But one morning, I started to gesture as I spoke. I looked at my hands and thought, "What am I allowing here? If I have to give up golf, what am I going to have to give up next?" I started finding out about things that can cause arthritis and certain other ailments, and began trying to correct my condition. I started to talk to my hands. And sure enough, they started to get better. They may not be things of great beauty right now, but I can open and close them. And I'm going to grab a golf club this afternoon!

If there is anything that just doesn't seem to respond, don't give up on it. Stay with it! If there are times when it doesn't seem to be working, ask yourself: "How can I be sure it isn't working?"

BELIEVE IN YOUR BODY

There is no such thing as the aging process in your body. Chronologically the years go on, but no cell in your body is older than fourteen months, so every cell of your body is practically brand new. How can it age?

"But," you say, "I see the same wrinkles, the same sag, the same kind of debilitation taking place. Where do they come from?"

From the consciousness. You have accepted beliefs that are now translated into the body. Give your body a break! Give it a chance to use those brand-new cells. They aren't all washed out and changed at the same time every fourteen months, but are continually changing. Let every cell that comes into your life be a new one. Welcome it in. Breathe the breath of life in it. Affirm the truth for it, and know that it is part of your whole, vital, beautiful, strong body. You will see the results. The law of cause and effect is always at work. Nowhere does it work any more graphically, specifically, and beautifully than in the working of your human, physical body.

There are many people who have been healed through prayer, but I could also tell you of others who have passed on, in spite of every kind of intensive prayer application. Why weren't they healed? We don't have an answer for everything, but we know the principle is right. Each of us has a cycle; each is here for a purpose. When the time comes, we will go on. But no one should ever go on out of surrender or hopelessness, or out of trying to impose his will upon God's will.

Affirm the good and perfect will of God. By instigating and following a program of creative, holistic life, you will experience all the good and all the blessings that life has for you.

Life

I'm alive with the joy of life,
I'm in tune with the song of life,
I vibrate with the energy of life,
I thrill to the beauty of life.

I give thanks for the gift of life,
I'm alert to the challenge of life,
I work at the business of life,
I happily play the game of life.

I cherish life,
I reveal life,
I love life,
I live life.

Thank you, Father
For Your Life in
My Life.[6]

PERSONAL REALIZATION

The free, full flow of Life is surging through me, awakening me, regenerating me, and filling me with the effervescence of pure Spirit. I am completely alive on every level and in every way. I experience vital aliveness in everything I am and in everything I do. I am spiritually attuned to Divine Reality. I am filled with the Holy Spirit. My mind is bright, sharp, and perceptive. My entire consciousness is sparkling and clean. I am attuned to the brightness and beauty of spirit.

I drink of the waters that He gives me, and I have in me a well of water springing up into Everlasting Life. My spirits are bubbling over. My "eye is single" and my entire being is "filled with Light" (Matthew 6:22). I am in tune with the Infinite.

My heart is beating in rhythm with the Heart of the Universe. My mind is attuned to the vibrations of Divine Mind. I am a channel through which the Glory of God flows forth. I am an instrument of perception, wisdom, and understanding. Vision, insight, and inspiration enliven my consciousness. The brilliance of the One Light fills my entire being.

The activity of Divinity fills my entire being. God is all of me. I am that part of God which I can understand. There is no place where God leaves off and I begin. I express the Infi-

---

6D. Curtis, "Life" in *Songs of the Soul,* p. 53.

nite in all that I am, and in all that I do. I am an unlimited being.

I am a native of Eternity. I live forever, one day at a time. I am an expression of Life, Light, Love, Power, Peace, Beauty and Joy. I am a perfect child of God. I am bright, beautiful and whole. And so it is.

Thank You, Father-Mother God.

CHAPTER 10

KEEP ON AN EVEN KEEL

An Oriental proverb says that God does not subtract from life the time we spend fishing. For fishing, I have at various times substituted many other activities—gardening, painting, writing, meditating, golfing, and even working. Yes, your work can be, and should be, fun.

The important thing is that you must have balance in your life. You must keep on an even keel, or you will tip over. Long before *stress, tension, pressure,* and *anxiety* became household words—and killers of the working populace—Shakespeare spoke out for balance in his "Speech to the Players," from *Hamlet:*

> Speak the speech, I pray you, as I pronounced it to you, trippingly on the tongue: but if you mouth it, as many of your players do, I had as lief the town-crier spoke my lines. Nor do not saw the air too much with your hand, thus, but use all gently; for in the very torrent, tempest, and, as I may say, whirlwind of your passion, you must acquire and beget a temperance that may give it smoothness. O, it offends me to the soul to hear a robustious periwig-pated fellow tear a passion to tatters, to very rags, to

split the ears of the groundlings, who for the most part are capable of nothing but inexplicable dumb-shows, and noise: I would have such a fellow whipp'd for o'erdoing Termagant; it out-herods Herod: pray you, avoid it.

. . . .

Be not too tame neither, but let your own discretion be your tutor: suit the action to the word, the word to the action, with this special observance, that you o'erstep not the modesty of nature: for anything so ov'rdone is from the purpose of playing, whose end, both at the first and now, was and is, to hold, as 'twere, the mirror up to nature; to show virtue her own feature, scorn her own image, and the very age and body of the time his form and pressure. Now this overdone, or come tardy off, though it make the unskilful laugh, cannot but make the judicious grieve; the censure of the which one must in your allowance o'erweigh a whole theatre of others. O, there be players that I have seen play, and heard others praise, and that highly, not to speak it profanely, that, neither having the accent of Christians nor the gait of Christian, pagan, nor man, have so strutted and bellowed that I have thought some of nature's journeymen had made men and not made them well, they imitated humanity so abominably.

. . . .

And let those that play your clowns speak no more than is set down for them; for there be of them, that will themselves laugh, to set on some quantity of barren spectators to laugh too; though, in the mean time, some necessary question of the play be then to be consider'd; that's villainous; and shows a most pitiful ambition in the fool that uses it.[1]

---

[1] W. Shakespeare, *Hamlet*, Act III, scene 2, ll. 1–15, 17–37, 40–47.

The Importance of Play

The idea of "diversion" is inherent in the concept of "play." It is essential that you learn how to turn your attention to matters that have no real importance or significance other than your wanting to do them and have fun. The scope of such activities is limitless, ranging from mountain climbing to crocheting and Scrabble. "Play" is anything you do for fun. It may actually be more intensive and strenuous than your daily work, but if it is fun for you, then you are playing. The only thing that is actually ruled out is your daily occupation of work, because one of the essentials of play is "abstinence or freedom from work."

You may say, "But I get more fun out of my work than anything else!" Fine! You should. Have fun working, but have fun doing other things, too. When your attention is held steadily upon one thing for too long, a lag develops, and you go stale. This is part of the law of reversed effort, which states simply that if you try too hard, the power works against you instead of for you. Play is a form of release that relieves tension and channels creative energy to work constructively. Play is a means of refilling. In play, you utilize aspects of yourself that are neglected in everyday activities.

Play, to be worth anything, must be a joyous expression of life. The arts, hobbies of all kinds, sports—both spectator and participating—travel, and the pursuit of the simple pleasures of nature, all offer a great field of play. Choose your form of play and have fun doing it. Play is an important part of life.

God and Golf

Golf, today, is classified as one of the major professional sports around the world. In the United States alone, several hundred professionals play tournaments over a ten-month period, with total prizes exceeding millions of dollars. In addition, there are hundreds of country clubs where thousands of members play golf, and an untold number of public courses where an even greater number of golfers play regularly.

Over the past 1,000 years (there are records of golf tournaments played in the 11th century), there have always been many who were dedicated to this challenging pastime. More people are playing golf (or playing *at* it) today than ever before.

What is golf all about? Even though it is classified as a sport, it really isn't. Nor is it a game. (A game is something you play for fun. Golf is often frustrating and exasperating. One weekend duffer threw down his clubs with an anguished howl, exclaiming, "And my wife thinks I am having fun out here!") It sometimes becomes addictive. Just a few hundred years ago, playing golf was deemed punishable by death by a reigning English king. The frivolity of golf was noted by a 19th century poem:

> The factory's near the golf course,
> And almost every day
> The children working,
> Can see the men at play.

Golf is often derided by nongolfers, "Look at those idiots chasing a little white ball, trying to knock it into a hole!" Why, then, do people play it? Writing as one to whom golf was once very important, I can only say that some fortunate (or unfortunate, depending on your point of view) mortals arrive at golf by natural evolution or selection. For some, golf provides a challenging way to develop high personal consciousness by growing spiritually, mentally, emotionally, physically, and psychically.

Golf is about life. Golf is a discipline. The difficulty is that there is no way of finding this out without playing golf, and there is no way of really playing golf until you find it out.

This paradox accounts for golf's unique place in human activity.

It is true that golf can be used to escape reality, but properly approached, it challenges us to perceive reality. Golf can provide no less than a way to find God. Therefore, it is deserving of attention by all spiritual aspirants.

Golf is not played against anyone or against anything. Golf is a matter of inner experience translated into outer expression. (Isn't that what life is?) The score of a round of golf, measured against "par" for that particular course, is merely an indication of how integrated and adept the player is. Par is symbolic of a certain expected standard of performance. Many players reach the standard and consistently exceed it. Others never approach par. It all depends upon the developed skill of the player working in coordination with the integration of the various levels of his consciousness during that particular round.

It's very similar to how we play the game of life, isn't it? To live life on any acceptable level at all, we must develop a certain understanding and skill. There are many variables on various physical and conscious levels. Each round of golf provides a score card that gives you vital information about yourself.

Consider such areas as: centeredness, relaxation, peace, harmony, freedom, attunement, visualization, concentration, coordination, integration, rhythm, discipline, focus, and timing. These are just some of the areas where you need to develop self-mastery in playing either the game of life or the game of golf. Actually, a round of golf is no less than "a slice of life." Golf is another way of telling you a lot of important things about yourself, and will give you constant reminders and challenges for improving and growing.

THE PRINCIPLE OF RELEASE

One further step is equally important and necessary for accomplishment: release. Let go and let God. After you have done all you can, it is time to let go and let it happen. Real accomplishment doesn't come about through your efforts alone. You need all the help you can get from the power that is greater than you are. Knowing when to cease from your personal efforts and turn your plans and projects over to the creative process to bring them to fruition is the secret of accomplishment.

The release principle is perfectly epitomized in the planting of your garden. First, you plan what kind of garden you want. Then you select the seeds and plants to accomplish your plan; you go to work to prepare the soil, digging it up, getting rid of rocks, lumps, and debris, raking and mulching the planting area. Next, you lay out the rows and hills to receive the seeds and plants and then do the planting itself. The final work step is to put the finishing touches on, smoothing the soil, perhaps fertilizing and watering. And then you are finished.

It is now time to stop and release it to nature to produce your crop for you. There is nothing more for you to do, other than whatever weeding, fertilizing, and irrigating may be necessary as time goes by. It is important that you completely release the seed and the plants and let them grow on their own. If you interfere with the gestation and growing process by digging and scratching around to see if your seeds and plants are growing, you will never have a garden. Do your part, and then let God do His part. Faith is a most important factor in growing your garden — and in living your life.

My father demonstrated his understanding of the law of release and the completeness of his faith, along with the necessity for hard work, on our wheat farm in eastern Washington. We all worked very hard to get the fields ready for seeding: plowing, harrowing, treating the seed, and then actually planting with horse-drawn drills. (Later we had tractors.) When we finished a field, removed our machinery, and closed the gates, my father would invariably say, "Well, boys, there's our crop for the year!"

He released it. He knew we had done all that we were required to do or could do. It was time to release the seed so it could grow toward the harvest. And, of course, barring flood, fire or drought (which sometimes did occur), the harvest always came. So it is with every project and endeavor in your life. Understanding the miracle of seed-time and harvest will keep your life in balance.

LEAVE SOME SPACE

When I became a full minister on my own, I kept a heavy schedule of intensive work. The work was there to be done; I enjoyed it; I was proud of the fact that I could do so much. Frankly, a lot of it was an "ego trip," but I didn't know that at the time, nor would I have admitted it if I had. I didn't even acknowledge the health risks and the strain on my marriage and family. But finally, I began to heed the counsel of my esteemed mentors, Ernest Holmes and Manly Palmer Hall, who had pointed out to me that work isn't everything—that other aspects of life need attention also.

"I don't understand why you work so hard," Dr. Holmes used to say to me. "You're one man trying to do ten jobs. Wouldn't it be better to get ten men to do ten jobs?"

Mr. Hall said, "There is something wrong if you are spending more than an average of eight hours a day at your work. You need to do a better job of planning. There are other things in life besides work, no matter how important and noble that work may be. I suggest you do somewhat as I do: when I have finished my eight or nine hours of writing and administrative duties (at his Philosophical Research Society in Los Angeles), I wrap it up, go home, and immerse myself in my collection of Japanese art, and experience pure *shibui* (the spiritual ecstasy, freedom, peace and euphoria that come from experiencing sheer beauty). As the beauty, harmony, and peace reach my soul, my spirit is healed and I am at peace. Or I go to my stamp collection, spend hours with it, and achieve the same result. Relax, son, the world is going to continue to spin without you spinning!"

On the morning of what was to to be the last day of her life, Hazel (Mrs. Ernest) Holmes' last words, as she bade me goodby and blessed me on my way, were, "Now run along and stop trying to fill every moment of your life. Leave some space between your appointments and your activities."

I understood what these beloved friends were telling me, but it took years for me to change, or even want to change. In the end, my approach has changed without my really doing anything about it. I have learned to handle whatever comes my way without getting all bent out of shape.

I am able to stay on an even keel by practicing the principles and techniques set forth in this book, the truths set forth in the Bible, the Ancient Wisdom, and many other modern New Thought and New Age teachings.

LIVING FROM WITHIN OUTWARD

After setting forth the principles of effective living in the Sermon on the Mount, Jesus concludes by saying:

> Therefore whosoever heareth these sayings of mine, and doeth them, I will liken him unto a wise man, which built his house upon a rock:

> And the rain descended, and the floods came, and the winds blew, and beat upon that house; and it fell not: for it was founded upon a rock.

> And every one that heareth these sayings of mine, and doeth them not, shall be likened unto a foolish man, which built his house upon the sand:

> And the rain descended, and the floods came, and the winds blew, and beat upon that house; and it fell: and great was the fall of it. (Matthew 7:24–27)

Jesus' instructions emphasize the importance of living from within outward, instead of the other way around. He directed: "Seek ye first the kingdom of God, and his righteousness; and all these things shall be added unto you" (Matthew 6:33).

You reach the inner center by establishing and maintaining balance and harmony inside yourself so that there is a perfect equilibrium between your inner being and your outer activity. This is accomplished by building an inner consciousness of calm, quiet, and peace, and adopting a way of life that expresses it. It will keep you "in the flow," and on an even keel. This inner harmony is best achieved through the practice of meditation.

Through my occult and esoteric studies, I practice techniques of meditation and make them an integral part of my spiritual life and what I teach. Meditation is the process of becoming one with life, one with being, one with all that is good, beautiful, and wonderful—becoming one with God. If you spend a good part of your day just running around doing "things," it stands to reason that you need to balance your activity with periods of contemplative thought when you don't try to do anything, but let something greater than you are do it through you.

"Meditation" comes from the Sanskrit word *meta,* which means *wisdom.* Meditation is "doing the wisdom," or "experiencing the wisdom." A synonym for wisdom, in this sense, is spirit, or light, or the presence of the infinite, invisible oneness.

It has been proved scientifically that the human body actually responds to relaxation and meditation. The blood pressure goes down, the heart beat is slowed, the pulse rate is quieted, the respiratory rate drops. A refreshing, replenishing activity of spirit starts to circulate through the entire organism, manifesting its perfection and wholeness.

Meditation is the process of beholding the Light in ourselves and in each other. Meditation is becoming still and knowing that the presence within is God; meditation is listening prayer. The basis of meditation is quietude. It is a process of prayer that is characterized by stillness. When the conscious mind endeavors to become still, there is an automatic response within us that quiets it down.

There is a mental law that says we become what we contemplate. Spend a certain proportion of your time in the contemplation of the infinite one, concentrating upon the divine presence within you with the expectancy that you will see God, become one with Him, and awaken to His Presence. The process is always from within outward.

When you meditate, you become "God-filled." In order to become God-filled, it is necessary to first become self-emptied. Use denials and affirmations; through self-examination, arrive at some decisions about what you want and don't want in your life, and prepare yourself for the greatest of all spiritual practices—the practice of meditation.

How to Meditate

Relaxation: Relax your body and sit easily in your chair with your spine erect and your head upright, in line with the base of your spine so that there is no slumping, but be relaxed in manner. Your feet should rest lightly upon the floor, or you may cross your ankles. Let your hands rest in your lap. Let go, release, and do nothing. Don't even try to meditate or think. Just be. Be receptive and perceptive to all that is bright and beautiful around you and within you.

Breathing: Just breathe easily. Don't "breathe in" as much as "breathe up." Breathe in through your nose, and feel the air going to the very top of your head. Then exhale easily through your mouth.

Since one of the key points of meditation is focus and attention, become aware of your breathing, because this helps you focus. You don't have to think of anything else; just breathe in and up, then breathe out, through, and down. Breathe: in, out; in, out; in, out. Breathe out through your mouth as though you were going to make the sound, *ah*. Breathe in through the nose and out through the mouth, lightly making the *ah* sound. Do this several times. Repeat the process, intoning *one*. Then again, making an O sound.

Intoning: Next form your lips a little differently. This time, you're going to intone *OM,* which is the universal sound, the God sound, the sound of the infinite. Breathe in easily, and intone *O-O-O-O-O-O-M-M-M-M-M.* Give equal value to the O and the M, intoning the O and vibrating the M. Once more: *O-O-O-O-O-O-M-M-M-M-M-M.* And again: *O-O-O-O-O-O-M-M-M-M-M-M.* Do this seven times, in a very easy, meditative manner.

Now establish the consciousness of breathing through your mouth, pulling the breath up from the very tip of your toes to the very top of your head, holding the breath centered there for a few moments before exhaling through the mouth. Do this several times.

Focus: In order to stay in a meditative, receptive state, the eyes are usually closed, but it is not absolutely essential. Attention to your breathing and to sound focuses your mind on specific spiritual activity within.

The next step is to focus your attention at the center of your forehead, and just let it dwell there. While you are mastering the techniques of meditation, adopt the following four progressive states of relaxation and receptivity.

Calm: Calm is upon the face of the deep. Affirm silently: *I am calm, cool, and collected.* Keep your attention at the center of your forehead. Meditation is not spoken; it is contemplation, concentration, and realization of spiritual truth. You may start by speaking, but then you will just become still and receive.

Quiet: Your attitude is one of receptivity and listening. Since the human mind tends to be very active, trying to do things on its own, you must quiet it down. You have something greater than your human mind—your personal will, which is one with the Father's will. Your mind can be willed to be still, so if it starts to wander off and think of outer things, just say, "This is not I." Just eliminate the intruding thought. The "I" that is left is the real "I am," which is God, Christ within.

Peace: Calm, quiet, peace. Keep the attention at the center of your forehead. Move from this into a feeling of total peace—the peace that comes from inner knowing, the peace that comes from being integrated, unified, attuned. Calm. Quiet. Peace.

Silence: Move now into a period of complete silence. You are in the midst of your meditation now. There is no time factor involved, no external concern or consideration. You are one with the One. Calm. Quiet. Peace. Silence. Sustain the silence now. In the consciousness of quietude, let "The God Chant" flow into your meditation.

The God Chant

O my God, my God, I love Thee,
How I love Thee, How I love Thee.
O my God, my God, I love Thee,
How I love Thee, my God.

God, God, God, how I love Thee,
How I love Thee, how I love Thee.
God, God, God, how I love Thee,
How I love Thee, my God.

(Repeat: Oh, my Christ, etc.)[2]

---

[2]Anonymous, in *Wings of Song* (Unity Village, MO: Unity School, 1984), p. 103.

Reflect upon its great affirmation, allowing it to penetrate your being as the silence is prolonged. You are now free in the realization of the oneness that transcends time and place, or distance, or space. You want nothing more than to be in the divine presence forever. What you have done in your meditation is to free yourself to come up to your natural level. You have come into the secret place of the most high, which you quest for, search for, and thirst for, more than anything else in the world.

You are now in the process of returning from the years of wandering in the wilderness. You are entering into the Promised Land, the Kingdom of God. Your humanity is functioning on a higher level than it ever has before. The more you practice the presence of God, the more you experience God.

Now, start to relate to the outer. Gradually stir a little, and begin to experience hearing and seeing again. Open your eyes just a little at first, and let the inner consciousness of oneness come to you. As you reestablish effective awareness, your deep inner experience of meditation is sustained in every part of your being. You have "asked in prayer," rather than in an external endeavor to cause something to happen; you have become still and let something happen, within. More answers, more solutions will come from the inner experience of meditation than any outer tussling could possibly give.

You never need to leave this place in meditation. Every meditation forms the beautiful, glowing essence of you, and then the world assumes its proper place in your experience. Once you have reached the heights in meditation, you can return there at will. Learn the technique of ten-second meditations. Wherever you are, whatever you are doing, you can always salvage ten seconds. Just make a short statement like, *The peaceful, orderly nature of Life is working through me now.* Then just sit absolutely still for a few seconds and let the inner force work through you as the inner power responds to silence.

Ideally, you will want to spend at least one hour a day in meditation, but you don't have to spend that long to start with. Begin with perhaps ten minutes, whatever you are comfortable with, aim toward twenty minutes in the morning, twenty minutes sometime during the day, and twenty minutes before you go to bed at night.[3]

Which is more real: the way you are right now, back with sense and contact, or when you broke that contact and floated freely in inner space? They are both real. You have two lives, the visible and the invisible, but they are One Life. That realization is the whole point of meditation. Learn how to sit quietly and peacefully and turn on the wellsprings of the great and magnificent potential within yourself. Find the inner joys and the great rich experience of silent meditation.

PERSONAL REALIZATION

I am calm, cool, and collected. There is perfect balance in my life. I know who I am, where I am going, and how to get there. I am in control of myself, and therefore I am in control of the circumstances of my life. I am completely integrated spiritually, mentally, emotionally, physically, and materially. I keep on an even keel. I am divinely guided, guarded, and directed.

I avoid extremes of all kinds. I believe in, and practice, moderation on every level of my life. I do not overdo anything. I keep everything under control. I balance work with play. I know there is a time for everything under the Sun. I have a significant part to play in the world, but "I of myself can do nothing. The Father that dwelleth in me, He does the work." This realization puts everything in perspective and keeps everything in focus. I know what is important and what

---

[3]Western students, especially beginners, are cautioned not to meditate too long at one time. Students brought up in the Eastern tradition can sustain longer meditations, but for Westerners, the shorter periods are sufficient. As you become accustomed to meditation, the periods can be extended.

is not. I concentrate on what is important, but I keep everything in perfect balance.

I do my work efficiently and well, but I do not let it consume me. I balance my work with play. I am regenerated and renewed by a wide variety of interests. I have a lively interest in everything and everyone. I participate, I observe, I experiment, I read, I study, I listen. The wonder and beauty of life flow into my consciousness and make me whole. I live totally on every level. The Universe is constantly revealing its miracles to me, and I drink them in with awe and wonder. I am a child of the Universe. I am a native of Eternity. I am a person for all seasons. My Universality balances my Individuality. I am poised and complete.

The free, full flow of life surges through me, making me whole on every level. I am bright in spirit, I am clear in mind, I am pure in heart, I am strong in body, I am ordered in all of my affairs. I embrace the good, the true, and the beautiful. My joy and faith make me whole.

I am a knower and a doer. I love music, art, literature, theater, and sports. I joyously participate in everything that life has to offer. I live life joyously and fully. My interests and hobbies provide the variety that makes the unity of my life possible. I am alive with the joy of life. Order, balance, harmony, and right action are with me all the days of my life.

In the silence and peace of meditation, I perceive and experience my Oneness with Life, with Being, with all that is good and beautiful and wonderful. Cosmic energies flow through me; the infinitude of Space fills me; the Universal Reality envelops me. I experience my Oneness with God.

Thank You, Father-Mother God. And so it is.

CHAPTER 11

THE BUSINESS OF LIVING

You are here in this life to live, to love, to learn, and to grow. These four areas constitute "my Father's business" as stated by Jesus in Luke 2:49. Be assured that there will always be something wonderful, meaningful, and inspiring for you to do. It is simply a matter of knowing your reason for being, fulfilling your purpose in life, and elevating random "busyness" to the realm of true "business."

Life is a great mystery and miracle. Living is the process of appreciating the miracle and exploring and coming to understand the mystery. Life is its own excuse for being. Life is for living.

Life is the universal spirit individualized in all things as the Living Christ. This is what Paul designates as "Christ in you, the hope of glory" (Colossians 1:27).

It is the ultimate potential of every atom and every vibration of being. The purpose of life on all levels is to release this inner light and energy into glorious outer expression.

God is Life. Living is the expression of God. God sleeps in the rock, stirs in the plant, expresses as simple consciousness in the animal, attains self-consciousness in man, and arises into full God awareness in enlightened man.

This means that all of God is present at every point of Creation at the same time. The Mineral, Vegetable, Animal, Human and Spiritual Kingdoms are all expressions of Life.

The level of life awareness on the different levels determines the nature and quality of living that each level expresses. We, who have self-awareness, have the potential of an unlimited level of living that lifts us into the spiritual kingdom of self-realization. Life lives itself through everything and everyone. With self-consciousness, we have the power of self-determination.

> So live, that when thy summons comes to join
> The innumerable caravan that moves
> To that mysterious realm, where each shall take
> His chamber in the silent halls of death,
> Thou go not, like the quarry slave at night,
> Scourged to his dungeon, but, sustained and soothed
> By an unfaltering trust, approach thy grave
> Like one who wraps the drapery of his couch
> About him, and lies down to pleasant dreams.[1]

LOVING

Love is the full expression of life. Life without love is just existence. Love makes the world go 'round. Love is the essence of living. Love is the dynamic force that originates life, and maintains and sustains it as a creative action. Love is the motivating force behind all purposeful endeavor. Love inspires. Love heals. Love is the desire of life to express itself. Love is dedication to purpose. Love is the language of the soul. Love is affirmative relationship to an idea.

If you have love, you don't need anything else. By the same token, it doesn't matter what else you have; if you do not have love, it isn't enough. You may be the smartest person in the world, the best artist, the best professional man, the

---

[1] W. C. Bryant, *Thanatopsis* (Chicago, IL: The Cable Co., 1929).

best speaker, the best musician; all will be of no avail unless you have love. Unless the soloist sings from a heart of love he or she might as well not sing. Unless the orator speaks from a heart of love, the message is empty. Unless the prayer pours freely from a love-filled heart, it does more harm than good. Unless you identify yourself with supreme good, you remain in isolation.

You must learn to love here and now. Love today — in the market place, on the street, in the home, at your place of business. Live today! Love today! Release past glories and past mistakes. Love today the power that God has given you. Love today the talent entrusted to your stewardship. Love today the people around you. Love today the ideas that come into your mind today. If you know how to love, everything else will come to you.

Do you love what you are doing? If you don't, nothing can come of it. The purpose, expression, love, and activity of a well-directed goal in life is the secret of love. Indeed, it is cooperation with the great love. If you love what you are doing, it will be successful and will come to fulfillment. If you despise your job, home, community, or anything else, each will be a total loss. Learn to love. Only in that way will a pattern be set up within you for larger experience.

Someone to Love

The first chapter of Genesis says, "God created man in his own image, in the image of God created he him; male and female created he them" (Genesis 1:27). This indicates that an individual is not complete until the male and female aspects of his or her soul are in perfect union with each other. Each of us has both male and female aspects of soul. You are not complete without union of the polarities within you. Woman is the soul of man; man is the soul of woman; the union is love. Until we find the union, we are always seeking for that other aspect of self.

One marriage ceremony states, "True marriage is the holiest of all earthly unions. True marriage is based upon a deep spiritual communion of two souls that find completion in each other." Life is incomplete unless you have someone to love. Your soul finds completion when you have someone to love. Ideally, of course, the completion is realized in marriage, where there is complete union: spiritual, mental, emotional, and physical, when you and your beloved are completely united. Many people are blessed in attaining it; others have not yet found perfect union. If you have, cherish it, guard, protect, and nurture it. If you have not, keep this goal ever before you and move constantly toward it.

Everyone needs someone to love in his or her life, and the first step to finding love is to become a loving person. Love life, love your true self, love your work, love all people — unconditionally. Your "finding someone to love" may go through many stages before you experience that perfect "You" you seek. There are many components of love in addition to union with another, and we need to experience all of them before true romantic love is even remotely possible. You don't find romantic fulfillment by seeking it as an end in itself. True union with another comes as the result of your becoming a loving person who gives unconditional love in every aspect of your life. To have love, be loving. You cannot lose that way, even though you may not find your perfect mate and "live happily ever after."

Loving is an ever-unfolding process that continues forever. Perfect romantic union with another person, as desirable and as important as it is, is only one of the experiences of love, and can only be sustained if both partners continue to grow spiritually and to deepen their quality of love, not just within the marriage, but on all levels of life. You cannot live without love. You cannot receive love without giving love. There is no other choice but to love.

Realize that you may not find your perfect mate during this lifetime, but continue to develop your capacity for giving and receiving love and keep moving toward your desired goal. Find something to love—a cause, a field of endeavor, a line of work, an avenue of expression—an immersion in the great wonder and beauty of life. Develop a lively interest in everything and everyone, and love will work its magic in your life.

Perfect Union

Go With Love.
Love! Love!
Let your heart take wings
    And fly to the farthest reaches
    Of inner space.

Go with Light.
Shine! Shine!
Let your soul radiate
    And shine away all of the
    Negativity of the world.

Go with Truth.
Know! Know!
Let the Christ of you
    Join with Father-Mother God
    In perfect union with the One.

Go with Life.
Live! Live!
Let yourself be that which
    God has created you to be:
    The expression of eternal life now.[2]

Steps for Finding Your Mate: In my capacity as a minister, I often counsel with both men and women who would like to be happily married, but just can't seem to get it put together. My counseling includes seven steps:

---

[2]Previously unpublished poem by D. Curtis.

1) Don't just focus upon what you want to get out of marriage. Plan what you intend to bring to it.

2) Make a list of all the qualities you would like to find in your ideal mate, and then go to work to develop those qualities within yourself.

3) Be loving in all relationships. Don't worry about receiving love, just be loving.

4) Give of yourself in every possible way, remembering that giving attention *to yourself* on every level is an important part of the process.

5) Develop a lively interest in everything and in everybody. This interest is love in action. Be interesting. Expand your consciousness spiritually, mentally, emotionally, physically, culturally, artistically, socially, financially, materially, universally. Be a part of everything and care about others.

6) Remember that there is the perfect mate who wants and needs you as much as you want and need him or her. Pray and work to become a perfect mate for that perfect mate, and know that the law of attraction is bringing you together.

7) Focus your spiritual disciplines upon these steps each day, and then release them and go about living your life joyously and fully. Let God provide what you need for your fulfillment, and give constant thanks for it.

Does this mean that everyone who follows this guidance manifests love and marriage? Love, yes, because the person who builds a consciousness of love, receives love. Romance and marriage? Not always. But if marriage is what you need for your complete self-realization, everything will be working together to bring it about.

You may not always obtain what you think you want, but you will always get what you need, whether you know you need it or not. The specific experience or circumstance may be necessary for you to learn certain lessons that are necessary for your unfoldment as a spiritual being. Give thanks for the lesson, no matter how painful it may be, and move steadily forward toward your goal.

Having someone to love may not necessarily lead to marriage, although an ideal marriage is beyond a doubt the highest human experience available during this lifetime. Since it is the highest experience that can come to you, it cannot be taken lightly. True marriages do not just happen, you "happen" them. The "they were married and lived happily ever after" myth is beautiful in fairy stories, but is not necessarily true. There is more to marriage than two people in love who want to be married, as beautiful and as essential to happy marriage as that may be. There must be commitment, and the realization that happiness in marriage must be earned and created. One marriage ceremony asks each partner to promise "to bring to the marriage the best that you have." When this promise is made and sustained, the marriage will succeed. If you don't bring the best that you have to it, there will be difficulty.

Marriage offers the greatest rewards, the greatest challenges, and the greatest opportunities, all in one package. A marriage is successful when both partners want it more than anything else, and are willing to work for it. The deplorable situation that more than 50 percent of marriages end in divorce indicates that these two requirements are not recognized, and the necessary effort is not put forth. There is a great need for education about marriage, before marriage.

INDIVIDUAL DEVELOPMENT

Development and maturation of the individual come first. The growth process must include spiritual values that will lead to the development of character and the expansion of consciousness. When two individuals who are on the path of

personal spiritual growth fall in love and make the commitment of marriage, and continue it in the marriage, it will succeed, because two whole units have come together to
complete a greater whole. However, if two incomplete and
immature individuals marry without recognizing what is involved, or do not recognize that marriage is a partnership
where each partner must continue to grow individually and
together, the marriage does not work out. When this is the
case, one of two things happens: there is a separation or divorce, or there is an unhappy marriage. Neither of these alternatives is good enough.

What to do about it? Start right now doing the best job
about yourself that you possibly can. Get with it! It is my
fervent prayer that the ideas in this book will be helpful to
you.

If you desire marriage and are working upon the seven
steps for finding love given earlier in this chapter, but still
don't seem any closer, keep on keeping on with your personal
program of making the most and the best of yourself. As you
do that, new insights, new avenues, and new experiences constantly open for you. It might be that you are not ready for
marriage, or that your destiny in this lifetime does not include
marriage. Both of these possibilities can be dealt with. If you
realize that you are not ready, embark upon a program following the suggestions given in this chapter and in this book.

If the realization comes to you that you may not experience marriage in this lifetime, do not accept this as defeat. Far
from it! Simply change your focus. Release the whole matter
into God's hands, and you will be at peace. With this peace
there will be a great flow of love through you. Your "someone
to love" becomes "everyone and everything to love." Conjugal
love is not the only form of love. The other avenues of love —
service, commitment to a cause, glorification of God, and
good works of all kinds — are not substitutes, but alternatives.
When you follow the Path all the way, it may happen that the
opportunity for marriage will come to you, and you can decide then whether you really want it or not. You can choose

whether you want one, the other, or both alternatives. You will know, because by then you will already be complete within yourself. Love is permanently your way of life.

For those who have made arrangements for marriage, a careful study of marriage and pursuing programs of personal spiritual growth are essential. It will bring you closer together. Your love will grow, and you will enter into your marriage with commitment and joyous expectancy.

For those who are married and are encountering difficulties, there is so much that you can do about it. Joining together in a plan to work on your marriage is the best way. But if you have grown apart, or were not really close in the first place, it may not work out at first.

Embark upon a personal program of self-development, understanding, and discipline. It may include counseling, classes, the study of books like this one, programs of self-improvement, and regular prayer, meditation, and worship. You will discover a great deal about yourself and about your marriage. Even though your partner may not join with you, he or she will notice the change in you and will appreciate it, whether it is mentioned or not. The wonder of it is that you will notice a change in your partner, who may even be inspired to embark upon a similar program. Or, your partner may ask to join you. Either way, it's a win-win situation.

Finally, be conscious of the effort it takes to make a marriage work. There are many guidelines for achieving a happy marriage and family structure built upon love and mutual trust and respect. Establish these steps and follow them:

1) Plan together.

2) Pray together.

3) Talk together.

4) Work together.

5) Play together.

LEARNING

Living is for learning. As you learn the lessons that life provides, you make it possible for more life to express through you. Life is a school in which you learn the lessons that enable you to live fully and abundantly. Some of these lessons are difficult, but they are essential for your unfoldment. Life affords you the opportunity to repeat your mistakes until you learn the lessons they alone can teach you. When you are confronted with challenges and difficult situations, ask yourself, "What is this trying to teach me?" Then apply yourself to learning the lesson so that you don't need to repeat the painful experience again.

Here are fifty lessons to test yourself on how your learning is coming along.

1. There is more to life than there appears to be.

2. That which is within you is greater than that which is in the world.

3. God's arms are around you and He is never going to take them away.

4. Nothing is as bad as it seems.

5. Everything is better than it seems.

6. No matter how bad things are, they always get better.

7. Nothing lasts forever—except life and love.

8. You can't hide anything from God and your real self.

9. You can't lie, cheat, or steal without destroying yourself.

10. "Good enough" is not good enough.

11. "Getting by" is getting nowhere.

12. You can't hurt another person without hurting yourself worse.

13. Appearances are not always what they seem.

14. No one can clean up your mess for you.

15. Love is the greatest thing in the world.

16. Everything happens for a reason.

17. There is no free lunch.

18. Every effect has a cause; every cause has an effect.

19. Prayer is talking to God. Talk to Him regularly.

20. More is not necessarily better.

21. There is no sin but a mistake; there is no punishment but a consequence.

22. Don't depend on anyone except God and yourself.

23. Don't ask anyone to do anything for you that you can do for yourself.

24. Get right on the inside and everything will be all right on the outside.

25. Take care of yourself and God will take care of you.

26. You're not nearly as good as you think you are. You're better!

27. If you think you know everything, you are proving that you know nothing.

28. There is more to be known than is known.

29. Hardly anything worth doing has yet been done.

30. "Trifles make perfection, and perfection is no trifle."[3]

---

[3] Reputed to be an adage translated from Michelangelo.

31. It is important to have an invisible means of support.

32. You are not punished for your sins; you are punished by them.

33. "What you are looking for you are looking at, and you are looking with."[4]

34. You always find what you are looking for.

35. Your worst fears never happen.

36. You always experience what you are.

37. What you believe always comes true.

38. You can't play in the dirt without getting some on you.

39. "Laugh, and the world laughs with you,/Weep, and you weep alone."[5]

40. "A merry heart doeth good like a medicine./A broken spirit drieth the bones" (Proverbs 17:22).

41. Smile, and you'll be smiled at.

42. "Let a fool hold his tongue and he will pass for a sage."[6]

43. You can't hide from yourself.

44. "Judge not that ye be not judged" (Matthew 7:1).

45. Self-castigation is a waste of time.

46. You can if you believe you can.

47. You live forever, one day at a time.

---

[4]E. Holmes, from a class lecture.
[5]E. W. Wilcox, "Solitude" in *One Hundred and One Famous Poems*.
[6]Publilius Syrus (1st cent. B.C.), Maxim 914.

48. If you don't like the way things are going, have a good talk with yourself.

49. "There's a divinity that shapes our ends,/Rough-hew them how we will."[7]

50. "We're all hell-bent for heaven by way of evolution."[8]

These are only a start. Check yourself out on this list, and then compile your own. You'll find that learning, just as living, is eternal. If you stop learning, you stop living. As long as you learn, you grow.

GROWING

Your growth depends upon the full development of your feeling nature. Extend your emotional horizons by incorporating the following seven feelings into your consciousness: love, faith, joy, peace, enthusiasm, wonder, and compassion.

Love: I have already discussed love to a great extent in this chapter. Here, I can only add that I believe love is the master emotion, which includes and indwells every other constructive feeling. The horizons of love are endless. It is impossible to love too much, so the business of life is to endeavor to love enough.

Love

From each warm embracing soul
Flows pure unadulterated love,
The elixir of life, the essence of being,
The very life of the Infinite Christ.

---

[7]W. Shakespeare, *Hamlet,* Act V, scene 2, ll. 10–11.
[8]E. Holmes, from a class discussion.

How wonderful these people are!
How bright, how beautiful, how dear,
Images and likenesses of God Himself!
My brothers and sisters, living expressions of
    myself.

Thank you, Father-Mother God for my human
    family,
Thank you for these rays of pure Light,
Thank you for these vibrations of pure Love,
Thank you for these expressions of God's Life.

We live, learn and grow together,
This current wave of God's children,
Sent by Him into this worldly incarnation
To share, enjoy and teach each other.

As we walk and talk together,
Every personal encounter is an adventure,
A privilege and an opportunity
To do more, see more and be more.

It seems to me that being a person
In a world full of beautiful people
Is God's greatest gift to His children.
Thank you, Father-Mother God, for my human
    family.[9]

Faith: This is a feeling that cannot conceive of its opposite.
There is no limit to what you can accomplish when your faith
is strong enough. Just as with love, it is impossible to have too
much faith. Believe in life, believe in God, believe in yourself,
believe in other people.

"Now faith is the substance of things hoped for, the evidence
of things not seen." (Hebrews 11:1)

---

[9]D. Curtis, "Love" in *Cosmic Awareness* (Dallas, TX: Christway Publications, 1984), p. 153.

"Things which are seen were not made of things which do appear." (Hebrews 11:3)

"If ye have faith as a grain of mustard seed, ye shall say unto this mountain, Remove hence to yonder place; and it shall remove; and nothing shall be impossible unto you." (Matthew 17:20)

"According to your faith be it unto you." (Matthew 9:29)

"Thy faith hath made thee whole." (Luke 17:19)

Joy: This is the soul quality of ebullience that gives lightness and effervescence to everything you experience. Let the vibrations of joy emanate from your soul, mind, and heart, and flow through your body and out into your world of activity.

"Make a joyful noise unto the Lord" (Psalms 100:1). Let the scintillating brightness of joy enliven everything you are and everything you do. Give everything the "light touch." Cultivate your sense of humor. "A merry heart doeth good like a medicine" (Proverbs 17:22).

Laugh a lot. If you need to learn to laugh, practice laughing until your sides ache. Every morning upon arising, hit the deck, strip down to the buff, stand in front of the mirror, and laugh for five minutes without stopping. This will neutralize all heavy influences, and will sustain your joy throughout the day. Do the same at night before you go to bed and before your final evening meditation.

Laughter establishes joyous perspective in your consciousness and helps you through any situation that may arise, not to mention its salutary effect upon your mind and body. Joyous thoughts and feelings actually heal your physical body with quickened vibrations that stimulate glandular secretions, improve circulation, balance metabolism, perfect digestion, and regulate elimination. All of this comes from joy. Joy is the great healer. Joy is the great creator. Joy is life at its highest vibration.

You can't fake joy, but you can develop it by following these suggestions: act as though you were, and you will be. Joy is both cause and effect. Singing is a great way to develop joyous feelings and attitudes. You can't sing and be miserable at the same time. Make up songs and melodies. God doesn't care whether you can carry a tune or not. God knows you only as a joyous being, filled with love and light. Joyously know it about yourself. Smile with this inner knowledge. Show joy upon your face and with your entire manner. Let everyone see how joyous you are. Smile! Laugh!

Abraham Lincoln was often grave and sorrowful because of personal concerns and tragedies, his awesome presidential burdens and responsibilities, and the tragic Civil War with its destructiveness, waste, and loss of life. But he always injected humor into the most challenging situations. In this way, joy bubbled up and the crises passed.

Jesus always inspired feelings of joy in his disciples, listeners, and followers, just as He does in our hearts today. As far as we know, He didn't tell jokes, repeat affirmations, or use techniques to make Himself joyous. He simply *was* joyous. He was joy, as well as being exemplary in every other way.

For most of us, however, it is advisable to develop joy inwardly and express it outwardly. Sing, laugh, run, jump, dance, and shout! Be joyous, and you will enjoy life. Enjoy life, and you will be joyous.

Peace: Peace is the pearl of great price. Attaining and sustaining inner peace of mind, heart, and soul are essential for happy, healthy, and successful living. There is no substitute for peace. Your peaceful consciousness is the cause of harmony in every aspect of your personal life—in your relationships and in all your activities.

Personal peace produces world peace. World consciousness is the aggregate of the consciousness of all those who live in the world. If there is turbulence and conflict in people's hearts, there will be turbulence and conflict in the world. Personal unrest produces troubled conditions in the world such as epidemics, crime, social and economic crises, and depressions. Violent weather conditions, natural disasters, and war are the direct result of violence and destructiveness in the consciousness of people.

The importance of your personal inner peace cannot be overstated. Make this your number one priority. The regular use of affirmations and the practice of prayer and meditation will anchor peace in your heart. Become poised and centered in pure spirit and let nothing disturb the calm serenity of your soul. Do not react to disturbing outer stimuli; act from the love and spiritual attunement within your inner being. Practice this sequence of progressive peace: Calm-Quiet-Peace-Silence. Listen to peaceful music, read poetry, pray regularly, meditate deeply. Think peace, feel peace, speak peace. BE PEACE.

"All things proceed from a quiet mind," says an ancient Oriental proverb. Jesus is often referred to as "the Prince of Peace." One of the eight great beatitudes says, "Blessed are the peacemakers, for they shall be called the children of God" (Matthew 5:9).

"Thou wilt keep him in perfect peace, whose mind is stayed on Thee" (Isaiah 26:3).

"Peace I leave with you, my peace I give unto you; not as the world giveth, give I unto you. Let not your heart be troubled, neither let it be afraid" (John 14:27).

"And the peace of God, which passeth all understanding, shall keep your hearts and minds through Christ Jesus" (Philippians 4:7).

Enthusiasm: This is one of your most powerful emotions. It means *from* or *in* God. Enthusiasm is the energy of spirit flowing through your will. Enthusiasm enlivens your entire being. It is the expression of your commitment, dedication, and "will-to-do." Not only does your enthusiasm amplify your powers, it is most contagious, and inspires others to follow your lead. Enthusiasm minimizes all difficulty and concern, and makes the most difficult task easy. Enthusiasm lifts all your endeavors to a higher octave. There is no opposing power when you are enthusiastic, because it is then that God is accomplishing all that you are to do, *through* you. "He performeth the thing that is appointed for me" (Job 23:14).

Keep your enthusiasm fresh and alive, and there will always be that within you that goes before you, "[making] the crooked places straight" (Isaiah 45:2).

Wonder: Feelings of awe and wonder inspire and motivate us as we are grateful for the magnificence of which we are a part. As our wonder at God and His universe expands, we become more grateful for the wonder of our own being. We exult: *Everything is wonderful (full of wonder)!*

How Great Thou Art

Oh Lord my God, when I in awesome wonder
Consider all the worlds thy hands have made,
I see the stars, I hear the rolling thunder,
Thy power throughout the universe displayed;

Then sings my soul, my savior God to Thee,
How great Thou art, How great Thou art![10]

Feelings of awe and wonder heighten our self-esteem and our feelings of worth in the great scheme of things. The wonders of the universe fill us with wonder, and we feel as Emerson felt when he said, "I, the imperfect, adore my own Perfect."[11]

Compassion: This emotion includes the feelings of love, sympathy, and empathy that we feel for others—human and oth-

---

[10]K. Boburg, "How Great Thou Art" from an old Swedish folksong, translated by Stuart Hines, 1899.
[11]R. W. Emerson, "The Over Soul" in *Emerson's Essays,* p. 318.

erwise. Compassion is love in action. Compassion is the ultimate form of "love thy neighbor as thyself" (Matthew 22:39).

Compassion is the tenderness that unites us with others. Compassion is more all-encompassing than pity, sympathy, or empathy. Compassion motivates us to sacrifice everything for the sake of others. It is putting their good above our own. "Greater love hath no man than this, that a man lay down his life for his friends" (John 15:13).

Something To Look Forward To

There are many teachings concerning the truth of reincarnation, with some variance among them, but they all agree in basic aspect: The soul exists continually, either incarnate or disincarnate. When it is incarnate (in body), we say that it is "incarnated" or "reincarnated." When your soul leaves this incarnation (when your body dies), it returns to the subjective state until such time as it becomes ready to resume objective (external) experience (to be reincarnated).

The process of reincarnation is called rebirth. Rebirth may mean a return to human existence, or it may be an embodiment on some other level of life expression that will provide the experience the soul needs for its growth and unfoldment. Since at our present level we can conceive only of humanness as our sole form of life, we do not know what other levels of life there may be. This we do know: reincarnation is part of the divine plan, known in the mind of God, and its components will be made known to us when we are developed enough to understand them. Rest assured that you will always exist *somewhere,* either incarnated on the human level or on some other level, either equal to or above it. You will never be reincarnated on a lower level of life, such as an animal or other creature (a theory that has sometimes been taught, but is refuted by enlightened teachers who have attained higher levels of understanding.)

Reincarnation is the integral corollary of the law of karma in Buddhism and other Eastern religious philosophies, and is simply known as the law (law of cause and effect) in Christianity. Even though this teaching is often refuted by orthodox and fundamentalist literalism, there are many passages in both the Old and the New Testaments that support it.

Karma: Within each of us, God's life is incarnated and embarks upon a path of individual experiences. The moment you were born, you started a sequence of karmic action—cause and effect—because you think. Every time you think, you set the creative power of life into operation.

The law of karma says: "Good deeds bring good results. Bad deeds bring bad results." *Karma* means *action*. The working of the law of cause and effect goes on forever. There is never a time when you have not existed; you are existing now; there will never be a time when you will not exist. Your destiny is to know God by loving God, by being one with God, by expressing God. If you do that, all questions will be answered, all problems solved, and all needs met.

Reincarnation comes from a Sanskrit word that means "to pass through intensely." This is what you are doing right now. You are passing through a life period "intensely." You are learning, growing, having experiences. This lifetime is but one of many lifetimes. You have lived before, and you will live eternally. As this world offers so many opportunities to learn and grow, what could be more appropriate than your soul, which is on an eternal journey, being born again into the circumstances of this world?

And you will keep creating karma, either good karma or bad. But actually, what we call "bad" karma simply means that you go through the results of negative, destructive, and selfish thoughts, and must learn lessons from them. So negative or "bad" karma also serves a purpose of good.

PEACE OF MIND

What does an understanding of the law of reincarnation do for you? It gives you perspective; it gives you peace of mind. It helps to explain some of the inequalities of life: the wide gap between rich and poor, between the intelligent and the ignorant, between the commonplace and the genius.

Treasures that have been stored up in heaven over an infinite period will develop naturally. Some of us are young souls; some of us are old souls, which simply means that we have had greater periods of growth and have developed greater understanding.

Understanding the law of reincarnation also helps you eliminate the bonds and bondage of the false, personal ego, the personality self, where attention is focused upon the personality. It inspires you to raise your consciousness to a higher spiritual level.

Fatalism is superstition. The laws of karma and reincarnation are the opposites of a belief in kismet or fate, which says that everything is preordained or predestined. Jesus and other great teachers (Buddha, certainly, and others of the Hindu religion) have taught that you can change your karma at any time.

You interfere with the law of karma intelligently by changing your choice: choose to give up certain habits; choose to follow certain directions; choose to pursue certain lines of endeavor or inquiry. In that way, your karma responds, and you rise above the law of averages.

Great peace comes into your life when you see these things in perspective. You were born into this world primarily as a sensory being; you have certain appetites, the first of which is hunger. There are other sensory and physical needs to be taken care of. Some people continue all through their lifetime on this infantile sensory level, without evolving. Gluttons, drunkards, and sensualists are punished—but not by anybody or anything in the outer. They are punished within their own bodies, within their own souls, within their own minds. They provide their own torture, suffering, and trouble through the working of the law of karma within their own consciousness.

Learn to eliminate destructive thoughts and actions. In many instances, you can see the results of your thoughts right now. Some of your thoughts and feelings, however, are more subtle; there is no immediate reaction. But wait. Just wait. If your thoughts are pure, if your feelings are warm, if your intentions are dedicated, if you have honest direction in your life, you are "laying up treasures in heaven." You are making deposits in the infinite bank account of life. "Though the mills of the God grind slowly, yet they grind exceedingly small."[12] There is always a surfacing of karma, some time, some way.

Now what good does this understanding do? First of all, it frees you from all kinds of superstition—such things as vicarious atonement as the way to heaven. Or trying to find salvation by undergoing a religious conversion or having someone perform a rite over you. Sincere as the people who engage in them may be, these are trivial superstitions.

When you learn to see your life in eternal perspective, you can take a lot of jolts—a lot of left hooks to the chin—a lot of being knocked down—because you know that you are growing through these experiences.

What you think, feel, and do today determines what you are tomorrow. What you are today is the result of what you were yesterday and yesterday and into infinity. You have come to this point in your eternal existence as the embodiment and expression of the sum total of what you have thought, felt, said, and done. This is the way the law of karma works. Reincarnation or rebirth is simply continuity.

12F. von Logau, "Retribution," a 17th-century work, translated by Henry Wadsworth Longfellow.

Rebirth: The true teaching of the law of reincarnation simply is that we are reborn—re-embodied. How often? It varies. Sometimes the soul is ready to return immediately. Sometimes it will live in limbo—dormant, refilling, reviewing, rebuilding, until it needs to be reborn. For a highly developed soul, there may be hundreds or thousands of years between incarnations, because it has developed to such a great point that it is continuing to evolve, build, and grow while in the subjective state of life.

Reincarnation is a basic premise in modern, enlightened New Age Teaching. You may either accept it or not. Fully understood, reincarnation is not an opinion, a belief, or a theory; it is a law and will, therefore, work as law whether you choose to accept it or not. There are many aspects of human life that cannot be satisfactorily explained without including reincarnation in your belief system.

However, if you believe otherwise, that is up to you. Undoubtedly, the most sensible course is to keep your mind open, "weigh and consider," and then go ahead in assisting your soul in its development by learning the lessons that come from experience, worship, and meditation.

You will never finish your work in this lifetime. If you could, you would have very meager goals indeed. Your goals will continue, and others will help you achieve them in other generations. You will be reincarnated into the world scene: when you are reborn, your karma will continue to work as the law of your life, just as it is now.

Evolvement: In your life right now, strive to evolve to the point where you choose to devote the major part of your energy, the major part of your time, to experiencing oneness with God. Don't wait. Start right now. Don't wait until you get tired of eating, or of all the pleasures that come to the flesh. Don't wait until you get tired of going to the office and working and accomplishing things and making a good salary and obtaining the good things of life. Don't wait to serve. Start right now!

Service is "good karma." Give to worthy causes; pray, meditate, think, study, correct your thoughts and get a wider viewpoint. All of these interpenetrate each other. You become a whole person.

Forget about results. Don't worry about whether you are going to heaven. You are going where you are going as the result of your consciousness—your thoughts, your words, and your deeds—your karma. There is no other way you can go. But if you want to go to a better place, do better things. Think better thoughts and feel better feelings, here and now.

The results of negativity return to you almost instantaneously. But so do the results of constructive thoughts and deeds. Build good karma in all that you do.

> Never the spirit was born;
> the spirit shall cease to be never;
> Never was time it was not,
> End and Beginning are dreams!
> Birthless and deathless and changeless
> remaineth the spirit forever;
> Death hath not touched it at all,
> dead though the house of it seems!
>
> Nay, but as one who layeth
> his worn-out robes away,
> And, taking new ones, sayeth,
> "These will I wear today!"
> So putteth by the spirit
> lightly its garb of flesh,
> And passeth to inherit
> a residence afresh.[13]

---

[13]"The Song Celestial" in the Bhagavad Gita, translated from the Sanskrit by Sir Edwin Arnold (London: Routledge & Kegan Paul Ltd, 1967).

PERSONAL REALIZATION

The warming, healing, blessing flow of Love surges through my entire being. I experience the Love of God on every level of my being—in every thought, feeling, and attitude. I am the recipient of Divine Love. I express unconditional Love. My life is filled with Love.

Love creates me, heals me, inspires, and blesses me. Love sustains, maintains, and strengthens me. God's arms are around me, expressing Infinite Love, and holding me close to the Creative Center of all Life. There is no place where God leaves off and I begin. I am One with Him in Whom I live and move and have my being. I am a perfect child of God. I am His Love Child. I am conceived in the Mind of God. I am created in the Consciousness of God. I am formed of the Body of God. I receive and I give the Love of God.

Love fulfills my life. I love the True Self of my being. The Christ of Love is the Light of my life. I love God, so I love myself. I love the Christ, so I love Life. I live Life lovingly, joyously, and abundantly. I am filled with Love. I love myself; then I love other people. God's Love is my love at all times. My soul is filled with Love. My mind is filled with Love. My heart is filled with Love. My body is filled with Love. My world of activities is a continuous expression of Love in all that I am and in all that I do. Love is the Law of my life.

My love for Life and for everyone is expressed in my work. "Work is Love made visible."[14] I love my work. I do all things to the glory of God. Through my work I give form and expression to the Universal Love that permeates everything. God's Love expresses through me in all that I am, and in all that I do.

The all-embracing Love of God beckons to me across the reaches of Eternity. Love is everywhere. Love is forever. I live,

---

[14]K. Gibran, *The Prophet* (New York: Alfred A. Knopf, 1967), p. 28.

love, learn, and grow with Love. Love is all there is. I am Love. Surely Love is with me all the days of my life, and I dwell in the house of Love forever. Thank You, Father-Mother God of Love. In the Name and through the Love of Jesus Christ. Amen.

CHAPTER 12

"TO THINE OWN SELF BE TRUE"

In Jesus' parable of the wise and foolish virgins, the kingdom of heaven is likened to ten virgins, who

> took their lamps, and went forth to meet the bridegroom. And five of them were wise, and five were foolish.
>
> They that were foolish took their lamps, and took no oil with them: But the wise took oil in their vessels with their lamps. (Matthew 25:1–4)

When the bridgroom came at midnight, the wise virgins trimmed their lamps and went to meet him. But the foolish virgins' lamps had gone out, and they had no oil. While they went to buy oil, the door was shut, and they were excluded.

Is this passage about virgins in the usual sense? Of course not! It is about consciousness. The "virgins" are a metaphor for your thoughts, feelings, and attitudes. The "bridegroom" is your ideal—what you want to be married to—what you want to achieve. Jesus is showing us here how important it is that you are "wise" (prepared) in your consciousness, and not "foolish" (unprepared). You "keep oil in your lamps" when you give your thoughts, feelings, attitudes, convictions, and senses constant positive input of conviction, expectancy, and affirmation.

Conversely, if you do not keep your "lamp" filled with positive expectancy, your "flame" (your hope and conviction) will go out and your "marriage" (your life's purpose) will not be consummated, no matter how hard you try to accomplish it by struggle and outer effort. The "bridegroom" only marries the "wise virgins" who are bright, beautiful, and pure from their "lamps" of high consciousness. The "foolish virgins" have missed their great opportunity, and no matter how they beg, they are rejected.

This beautiful lesson reminds us that consciousness is the only reality. You are responsible for your own destiny. The choice is up to you. You can fritter your life away in foolishness, or you can keep oil in your lamp (consciousness), achieve your goals, and enjoy all that life has to offer. In a very real sense, you will be "married" (to your ideal) and "live happily ever after." Be a "wise virgin!"

Jesus is the master motivator. He "tells us the way it is":

> For the kingdom of heaven is as a man traveling into a far country, who called his own servants, and delivered unto them his goods.

> And unto one he gave five talents, to another two, and to another one; to every man according to his several ability; and straightway took his journey. (Matthew 25:14, 15)

The servant who had received the five talents invested them to yield five more; the servant with the two as well. But the servant with only one talent fearfully buried his talent in the earth. When the master returned, he rewarded the first two with high praise:

> Well done, thou good and faithful servant: thou hast been faithful over a few things, I will make thee

ruler over many things: enter thou into the joy of thy
lord. (Matthew 25:21)

But he severely reprimanded the one-talent servant and took
away what little he had.

This parable is also a lesson in consciousness. It motivates you to examine yourself and determine your level of consciousness: one talent, two, or five. The story tells us that the
"man" (life) entrusts his "servants" (capacities) with responsibilities that correspond to their consciousness (capacity to
achieve). Each is given "according to his several ability": one,
two, or five talents. Then the man travels "into a far country,"
and the servants are left on their own to accomplish whatever
they can.

Remember, this story is about you and me, and tells us
exactly how the law (the creative action of life) works. Consciousness is cause; achievement is effect. The "two-talent"
and the "five-talent" servants double their money because
they do their very best to make the most of themselves. The
"two-talent" servant does not have as much native or developed ability as the "five-talent" one, but he has an equal understanding of the law. Both are rewarded by life, in exact
ratio to their consciousness and the effort they put forth, just
as you and I are.

This leaves us with the "one-talent" servant who hid his
"talent" (consciousness, ability, and effort) "in the earth"
(darkness, ignorance, materiality), accomplishing nothing
whatsoever, and had to start all over again to learn life's great
law: "For unto every one that hath shall be given, and he shall
have abundance: but from him that hath not shall be taken
away even that which he hath" (Matthew 25:29). Be a five-
talent person!

These two parables tell you all you need to know in order
to reach the conviction that whatever you set out to do, you
can do. There is nothing you cannot be, do, and achieve if
you want to—if you develop the high consciousness that is
necessary to do it. Read these two parables again, realizing

that they are about you and have a special, personal message for you. Meditate upon them; ask your inner teacher to tell you what they mean and how to apply their lessons to your life. The truth that is revealed to you will lift your consciousness to new heights. You will be prepared to fully accomplish what you have set out to do.

> This above all: to thine own self be true,
> And it must follow, as the night the day,
> Thou canst not then be false to any man.[1]

You were born with certain tendencies, talents, and characteristics. All but your basic nature can be changed. You can change the way you think, the way you feel, the way you look. Your inner consciousness holds the key.

THE SEVEN RAYS

All life, light, and energy come from the One Source, the First Cause and Creator of the Kingdoms of Nature: the mineral, the vegetable, the animal, the human, and the many levels of the enlightened human and spiritual kingdoms.

Light and energy are radiated out from the Sun throughout the solar system into all the planets and all created manifestation, through the Seven Rays. Each ray dispenses a specific type of energy which determines the characteristics of the individual manifestation, human or planetary. For instance, the planet Earth is on the Second Ray of love-wisdom which it is to develop during this phase of its evolution. As the custodians of the Earth, the human kingdom is also on the Second Ray, although it is filled with individuals who are on all of the different rays. The person's predominant ray determines his personal characteristics and energy focus during his current incarnation.

---

[1] W. Shakespeare, *Hamlet,* Act I, scene 3, ll. 77–79.

An understanding of the Rays helps you understand yourself so that you may experience maximum unfoldment during this incarnation, and your knowledge of and cooperation with the Rays is the key to your destiny.

There are seven rays that indicate seven major levels of expression and endeavor:

1) Will and Power.

2) Love and Wisdom.

3) Active Intelligence.

4) Harmony through Conflict.

5) Concrete Knowledge and Science.

6) Idealism and Devotion.

7) Ceremonial Magic and Order.

Each of us is a composite of all seven of the rays. The two predominant ones are the Personality Ray and the Soul Ray. Since the Personality Ray is the most obvious and recognizable, it is called the primary ray. The Soul Ray, not as readily outwardly discernible, is called the secondary ray.

Knowing which ray you are on helps you determine your direction in life and the field of endeavor through which you may express. You may have aspects of all seven of the rays, but when you are honest in your self-examination, you find that one predominates, and a second is definitely indicated. You have a primary ray and a secondary ray; your primary ray motivates you toward your occupation, while you secondary ray determines your avocations, hobbies, and special interests. Your secondary ray is supplemental to the primary, and serves to balance your primary tendencies. It may be helpful to you in determining an alternate occupation. A spiritually developed individual will have tendencies of all the rays.

One of the results of spiritual maturity is the strengthening of all the rays in your consciousness. The following will help you on your pathway of ray development.

Will and Power: The First Ray is the power ray. Individuals on this ray have a strong personal ego and a strong personal will. They are highly motivated, and have a dynamic which often sweeps everything along before it. First Ray people have no difficulty in determining their purpose, or what they think is their purpose in life, and let nothing stand in the way of achieving it. They know what they want; they organize and plan their lives, and are definitely goal-oriented. They have unbounded energy, and will often set a pace that outdistances the field. They are definitely achievers (often over-achievers), and work hard at being winners. People on this ray are ambitious, and are often workaholics.

The First Ray provides us with the world's leaders: executives, managers, entrepreneurs, developers, business tycoons, politicians, military officers, and leaders in many other fields of endeavor where individual initiative is required. If you need to get something done, enlist the aid of bona fide First Ray individuals, tell them what you want them to do, and get out of the way. First Ray people are the doers of the world.

As with all of the groupings, First Ray tendencies must be kept in balance. So if you recognize yourself as a First Ray person, pay particular attention to your forceful tendencies. You must be on guard against being overly aggressive and throwing your weight around. You must realize that you can't always have your own way. Or, if you insist upon having it, that there are ways to get it other than beating the door down. You must understand that you are not always right. Should you stubbornly insist that you are, expect a lot of opposition to your egotism.

As valuable as First Ray people are to the world and to the progress of civilization, they can be a colossal pain in the neck. First Ray power has been responsible for much of the world's progress, but it is obvious that First Ray tendencies have caused conflict, aggression, conquest, and war, since time began.

If you are a First Ray person, what are you to do about yourself in order to avoid negative imbalance? The answer is obvious: develop the balancing and compensating tendencies of the other rays. Remember, you have qualities of all the rays, even though many of them are dormant and inactive. Awaken them and weave them into your makeup. This may well be part of what Paul was talking about when he directed, "Be ye transformed by the renewing of your mind, that ye may prove what is that good, and acceptable, and perfect, will of God" (Romans 12:2).

I am a First Ray person, or so I have been told by perceptive spiritual teachers. I recognize that I have most of the First Ray qualities, and that I have allowed a good deal of First Ray imbalance to develop in my life from time to time. But in spite of this, my self-concept includes certain qualities from all of the seven rays. Of course, this is not only true of me, it is true of you.

Developing the supplementary tendencies from all seven rays will make you a spiritually mature, balanced individual in personality and soul. Compensate for personality tendencies which may be causing you trouble by developing your soul.

For instance, since I am a First Ray person, it is necessary for me to pay particular attention to developing my Second Ray aspects of love and wisdom, so that a balance is established. Having been aware of this for some time, I assiduously endeavor to temper my forcefulness with love and wisdom. I am therefore happier within myself, I get along better with other people, and my First Ray efforts are more effective. I also have highly developed Fourth and Sixth Ray tendencies, which account for my involvement as a spiritual teacher.

The rays reinforce each other. Upon examination of yourself and others, you will be fascinated to see how each is a composite of the ray energies formulating and activating your life. Study these guides to the rays, and you will be able to change your consciousness, which will in turn change your life.

Love and Wisdom: It is necessary for everyone to be aware of the importance of developing the Second Ray aspects on both the personality and the soul levels. There is nothing more important than being a loving, kind, caring individual. If true, all-embracing, unconditional love is part of your makeup, everything else will work out. If the outer experiences of your life should not always be what you desire, it really won't matter, because the love within you is your greatest good and your highest achievement. There is nothing greater than love. Love is your greatest soul quality. Jesus' two commandments concerning love, "Thou shalt love the Lord thy God with all thy heart, and with all thy soul, and with all thy mind. This is the first and great commandment. And the second is like unto it, "Thou shalt love thy neighbour as thyself" (Matthew 22:37–39), indicate three focal points for the expression of love: God, yourself, other people.

When you love God, you will automatically love everything else, because God is All-in-All. There is only one law governing all human behavior: Do as you please, but first, love God. When you love God you cannot possibly lie, cheat, steal, kill, or behave in an unseemly manner. Love for God is the cause of exemplary behavior, the source from which all love flows. "We love . . . because he first loved us" (I John 4:19).

Love is a way of life. There is no such thing as being a little bit loving. You can't love partway. Unless your love is unconditional, it is not love. Love transforms your life. Love gives purpose and meaning to everything you do. All love starts with loving God.

If you don't love yourself, no one else is going to. This, of course, is not self-centered egotistical narcissism; it is just the opposite. Complete love includes love for your real self, which you are and which you can become in full expression. Love is complete affirmation. Love transforms, heals, motivates, and guides and directs you. Love for God and love for yourself are reciprocal. If you love God, you cannot help loving yourself, because you are made in the image and likeness of God. As you truly love yourself, you will go to work to eliminate any unlovable personality and character traits. Develop yourself as a loving person by loving. Observe yourself to see how you may be unloving. Stop doing those things, and start loving. It's as simple as that!

You may say, "But that's hard to do!" Maybe, but since love is essential, you have no choice but to become loving—and that includes loving yourself.

You can only love others if you first love yourself. Love for others does not necessarily imply affection or approval—you can love people without liking their behavior or what they have done with themselves. Love enables you to see through the facade of the individual to the perfect self within. Love beholds the Christ within a person, and enables you to see him or her as a child of God, and therefore your brother or sister.

Love dissolves any tendency to condemn, criticize, hate, hurt; or any desire to punish or get even with another. Love is an empathic response to others that enables you to identify with them, treat them in a considerate manner, and help them. You will be greatly helped in doing so if you just remember, "There but for the grace of God, go I."

How would you feel if you thought that God could or would stop loving you? How can any of us possibly feel that we have the right to withhold our love from others, no matter how unlovable or how separated from God they may seem? Jesus set the absolute standard for human relationships when He instructed: "Love your enemies, bless them that curse you, do good to them that hate you, and pray for them which despitefully use you, and persecute you" (Matthew 5:44).

Expression of love in these areas indicate a strengthening of your Second Ray aspects, and is a major step in your self-improvement and spiritual fulfillment. The requirements for every individual human life are: self-improvement and service to others. Both make the world a better place in which to live, and are the way we repay God for giving us life.

The second aspect of your Second Ray development is wisdom. Proverbs says, "In the lips of him who hath understanding, wisdom is found" (Proverbs 10:13). "Understanding" is "standing under" God's law, which is the ultimate wisdom just as it is the ultimate law. The love and wisdom of the Second Ray are one and the same: love is the awareness of the presence of God in your life; wisdom is the awareness of how love is the ultimate guide and fulfillment for all individual endeavor.

There can be no real achievement or fulfillment for anyone without the full development of the Second Ray. With that development, everything else falls into place. The remaining five rays are guides to help you understand yourself better and guide you in recognizing your purpose in your life, in making plans and setting goals, in engaging in those endeavors, and doing the work which you came into this life to do.

Active Intelligence: The Third Ray joins the first two in forming the trinity of the three basic aspects of individual human beingness. Intelligence is instilled in us as part of the creative process that brought us into being. We are created out of the infinite intelligence that is the first cause of all things; therefore, we are intelligent. We are knowers. We are capable of thinking, learning, reasoning, comparing, observing, relating, correlating, measuring, synthesizing, growing, integrating, and creating. We are individualized expressions of divine mind (God). What is true of God is true of us. We are the microcosm; God is the macrocosm. God is the great; we are the small. There is no place where God leaves off and you begin. Affirm: *God is all of me. I am that part of God that I can understand.*

All that is known or has ever been known is in the mind of God, and therefore in your mind; because you are "a point of light within the Mind of God." Your mind is an instrument through which the Mind of God thinks. What is true of God is true of you. Whatever God can do, you can do, because you are one with God.

There you have it—the essence of the Third Ray. Know it consciously, and use the infinite intelligence that is at your command. As you expand your individual consciousness, more of your infinite spiritual potential becomes activated. Remember, "a mind expanded to the dimensions of a greater idea cannot return to its original size."

As you concentrate upon developing the aspects and attributes of the Seven Rays, all limitations are dissolved from your consciousness, and you become a fully functioning creative instrument of the creator. You become nothing less than God in action!

We are still only at the dim dawn of time as far as our true potential is concerned. We have not even started. All the equipment has been installed within us, but we have not yet become acquainted with it or really used it.

God created us in His image after His likeness, and gave us dominion over all the earth (Genesis 1:26). The trouble is that for the four million or so years of our existence on this planet, most of our attention and effort has been toward extending that dominion over all the earth, without even beginning to establish dominion over ourselves. Our history, therefore, has been a painful one, simply because the major thrust has been outer rather than inner. The imbalance has brought us to the brink of total annihilation. With this threat we are forced to change our focus to our inner being, where the infinite itself resides.

You recognize, I am sure, that development of the Third Ray of active intelligence within you, along with the Second Ray of love-wisdom, is the answer. These aspects of the human potential have been largely ignored, while the focus has been on the First Ray of power and personal will.

The true direction is given in the Bible: "Not by might, nor by power, but by my spirit, saith the Lord of hosts" (Zechariah 4:6). All of this can be resolved when you start to think of yourself as a spiritual being with unlimited potential, and concentrate on developing your Godlike (spiritual) qualities. It is not too late. The place is here; the time is now. Take yourself in hand. All you need to do is establish your point of intention, decision, and action, and God will do the rest through you. Recognition and understanding of the seven rays is a major part of the process.

Harmony Through Conflict: The following ancient invocation indicates our progressive unfoldment into higher levels of soul development.

> Out of darkness into light,
> Out of ignorance into enlightenment,
> Out of death into immortality.

Our spiritual progress is dependent upon our mastery of the mystical alchemy, which, allegorically, transforms base metals into gold by the mixing of certain ingredients and finding the philosopher's stone. The ancient teaching of transmutation, transformation, and transfiguration, given by medieval philosophers as a symbolic formula for human regeneration, was taken literally. Many searched diligently for the alchemy that would make them rich by making gold out of inferior substances. These efforts were, and continue to be, ludicrous.

Humanity is still looking for shortcuts to attaining the rich rewards of life without practicing the prerequisite spiritual disciplines, and we are continuing to find that it cannot be done.

The Fourth Ray has a great deal to do with your spiritual development. You have seen how problems and difficulties (which we call challenges) are an integral part of human experience. You must learn how to transcend them. The Fourth Ray attribute of achieving harmony through conflict recognizes that "it is better to light one candle than to curse the darkness."[2] There are far too many people ranting and raving against "outrageous fortune" and doing nothing about it. You can achieve harmony through conflict when you realize that there is a perfect pattern in the mind of the infinite for all things known. You have the capacity to bring yourself and all things in your world into alignment with that perfect pattern.

The practice of meditation helps you achieve that realization. All artistic endeavors—music, poetry, painting, sculpture, dance, drama, architecture, and design—release the "imprisoned splendour" into outer beauty.

You can do it! Develop your Fourth Ray, and the results will appear in your life.

Concrete Knowledge or Science: Of course, it is one of your human attributes to find out about things. Your mind is naturally curious. It seeks knowledge and information so that it may correlate the data, thus forming the basis for understanding and efficient functioning. Through observation, experimentation, and experience, the mind discovers principles and laws that lead to comprehension of the world and the universe.

> To see a world in a grain of sand
> And a heaven in a wild flower,
> Hold infinity in the palm of your hand
> And eternity in an hour.[3]

Thus it arrives through inductive reasoning at the same point of wisdom and understanding that is reached deductively on the Sixth Ray through faith and intuition.

---

[2]Motto of the Christopher Society.
[3]W. Blake, "Auguries of Innocence" in *English Prose and Poetry* (New York: Ginn & Co., 1907), ll. 1–4.

Fifth Ray people love details, facts, and figures. They like to deal with things; external tangibles and material phenomena. The more minute the point of focus, the better they like it. They are empiric and thorough, meticulous and disciplined in all things; dedicated to doing a good job. Even though a Fifth Ray individual may develop tunnel vision through constant focus on external things, it is most important to develop the quality of this ray so that order and balance are established in your life design.

This is the ray of the scientist, who needs idealism, faith, and wisdom (see Rays Two and Seven) in order to attain balance, just as every one of us needs to develop Fifth Ray disciplines and methods. All of humanity owes a great deal to science, its discovery and development of mechanical and technical areas and advances in medicine and health care. However, science must be balanced by spiritual values, just as the predominant ray of every person must be supplemented by all the other rays.

Idealism and Devotion: While all Sixth Ray people are deeply religious (or spiritual), it does not necessarily follow that they must be involved with organized religion. All too often, the mystical sense is stifled by formal religious theologies and organization. The Sixth Ray person is primarily centered in religion, but only in the sense that the religious or spiritual aspect of life is of primary interest to all, whether we are consciously aware of it or not. It would be safe to say that all those in religious professions who have contributed to the spiritual betterment of humanity are on the Sixth Ray.

Mystics, saints, idealists, philosophers; many ministers and teachers; and inspired writers, poets, artists, and musicians are Sixth Ray individuals. It is the Sixth Ray people, along with the Second Ray ones, who keep humanity focused upon the true purpose, richness, and meaning of life. These are the two rays that provide the energies that lift us into the dimensions of our true potential. Developing love and sensitivity to the higher values of life will give us reverence for all life, and activate the intuition so that we are able to receive direct guidance from within.

Ceremonial Magic and Order: Creative thinkers and organizers are on this ray. The energies of all the other rays are integrated in this one, giving form and organization to purposes, plans, and goals. The Seventh Ray person is dedicated to individualizing the universal so that its reality may be seen and used. They transmute thought into form and action, and persevere until their objectives are attained. As you develop your Seventh Ray, you will have the strength, courage, and self-reliant faith to be true to your purposes and goals until you achieve them.

Follow these brief guides to the development of the universal spiritual energies that are active within you; integrate them, and you will always know where you are going. It is the purpose of this book to give you the tools, the techniques, the understanding, and the inspiration to enable you to do so.

WHATEVER IS TRUE OF GOD IS TRUE OF YOU

When you sing, praise, and recognize the reality that is God, you are really affirming: *Whatever is true of God is true of me.* How can we make such a statement? Think of God as being the macrocosm. Think of yourself as an individualization and likeness of God in all that you are and all that you do. You are a child of God. "Trailing clouds of glory do we come from God, who is our home."[4]

The Genesis story tells us that God "formed man of the dust of the ground, and breathed into his nostrils the breath of life" (Genesis 2:7). This does not mean, literally, that God scooped up a handful of dust and breathed life into Adam.

---

[4] W. Wordsworth, "Ode: Intimations of Immortality from Recollections of Early Childhood," ll. 65–66.

The Bible is allegorical, Jesus gave many of His teachings in parables. The allegory in Genesis tells us that God took a part of Himself and shared it with each of us. That is why you are potentially God. God asleep is human; a human awake is God.

The teaching of the New Age is to awaken us to our full potential, to awaken us to infinite possibility, to awaken us to our divine reality—to release the dynamic we each have within. You have the gift of conscious choice; God could not make you in His image and likeness without giving you freedom. Therefore, you have the freedom to make your own mistakes, the freedom to seek the answers to your questions. You have the freedom to solve your own problems. You have the freedom to act in any way you want, as long as it does not interfere with or harm others.

Your consciousness is always externalizing itself. Never compare yourself to others, nor try to assess the value of what you are or what you are doing; seek to be and do your best. The beauty of a great artist comes from the beauty in the soul of the artist. The violence in the life and reign of a conquering king comes from his soul. Consciousness externalizes. If you contemplate beauty, looking upon the inner side of things and endeavoring to become one with the consciousness of God, that beauty will externalize.

A king is a king because he has the consciousness to be a king. A saint is a saint because he or she has a saintly consciousness. You are a great builder or designer, you change the course of history, because of your consciousness, not because you are contemplating your position in history; and not because you are building something that will some day be thought of as the biggest or the greatest or the most beautiful. The real beauty of life is the constant development of consciousness.

Learn the lessons of the past. Those who have gone before, whether they were warriors, lovers, sinners, saints; whether they carved things out of the side of a mountain or delicately painted them upon a canvas; whether they were artists of living or artists of doing; whatever it may have been, they have all contributed to what you are.

Woven into the warp and woof of your life is everything that has ever come before. In your own subjective mind, you are the repository of all things that have ever been done, and of all the great and beautiful things that have ever been said, painted, expressed, or sung.

Dimensions

There are higher levels of consciousness
Than I have ever known.
There are more fertile seeds of awareness
Than I have ever sown.

There are more wonderful places
Than I have ever been,
There are more dimensions of time
Than now and then, ever or when.

There are more beautiful people
Than I have ever met,
There are more planets, moons or suns
Than I have seen rise or set.

There is a greater God
Than I have ever prayed to,
There are more worthy goals
Than I could ever aspire to.

There are more worlds to conquer
Than I have ever sought,
There are more precious treasures
Than I have earned or bought.

There are more noble prizes
Than I have ever won or lost,
Life has experiences to give me
More valuable than any cost.

Heaven is mine for the taking,
Christ waits within for my knowing,
The appearance of God's perfect child
Awaits my awareness and showing.[5]

When you become quiet and still and open your mind and heart to the influence of nature, of love, of joy, of song, of prayer, you become a channel through which beauty is expressed. To be your own self is the greatest beauty there is; to do what you are guided to do; to live from inner inspiration of your higher self. Let your voice be the voice of something that is clearer, more incisive, and more beautiful than you ever imagined.

Beauty doesn't come from building out of granite, marble, stone, steel, or glass. It comes from building a strong soul. The great creative power will take care of the rest. The great and wonderful challenge of life is to stay close to the creative source, to clearly see that you are important, wonderful, and beautiful.

Life itself is the masterpiece of God. Life itself is the most beautiful experience of all. Life is for living. Live your life fully every moment of every day. It's up to you!

Personal Realization

Everything unlike the Nature of God is dissolved from my consciousness now and forever. I am true to God. I am true to myself. The free, full flow of Divine energy is flowing through my entire being. I am a child of the Universe. I am a native of Eternity. I am a full and complete expression of the One.

There is One Life. This Life is God. This Life is whole. This Life is perfect. This Life is my life now.

I release the past. I embrace the present. I praise and bless the future. I give thanks for all experiences of the past

---

[5]D. Curtis, "Dimensions" in *Cosmic Awareness,* p. 65.

which have taught me the lessons I need to know as I move forward through Eternity. Everything that is good is permanently etched in my consciousness. Everything else is dissolved. I am free from all limitation as I live fully in the here and the now. I am a perfect Child of God, and it does not yet appear what I shall be as I move inward, upward, and onward along the Pathway to Perfection. I move forward into the future with enthusiasm and expectation of good.

My consciousness is high and my character is strong and exemplary as I dissolve all vestiges of my false ego and affirm and strengthen my true Ego — the Christ within me. I am created in the image and likeness of the Perfect Self, and I devote my life to achieving the expression of It. I am a spontaneous creative action of Spirit, which is individualized in me. I am a spiritual being going through a human experience on the way toward the complete and perfect unfoldment of my Real Self. There is nowhere God leaves off and I begin. We are One. I am true to the One.

I am here in this life to live, to love, to learn, and to serve. I am an individualized creative action of God. I worship God by giving and serving. I give of myself freely and joyously for the good of all. God has given me everything. I show my gratitude as I give all that I can to whomever I can, whenever I can. In service, I dedicate myself as an open channel through which the loving, creative activity of God flows forth and makes this world the Kingdom of Heaven.

I live in this kingdom — now, and I do all that I can to help others do the same. This is my purpose in life. I am true to this ideal.

Today

Welcome bright new day!
With great expectancy and joy,
My mind and heart are ready
For everything that you will bring.

Gone are the cares of yesterday,
As even its memory fades,
And I am ready for all
The things that are ahead for me today.

Today is the first day
Of the rest of my life.
Today is the best day
That I have ever known.

I may not know what
Lies ahead of me this day,
But I do know that God is with me,
And it can only be good.

I go forward into this day
With unbounded enthusiasm.
Filled with inner peace and gratitude
For the abundance God has given me.

This is my day. I live it fully.
This is God's day given to me
To do my best and to be my best
As I go about His business.

Every moment of this day
Is an opportunity to do God's work
With kind words and loving hand,
Helping others along the way.[1]

---

[1]D. Curtis, "Today," previously published in *Songs of the Soul,* p. 73.

Appendix

Several books have been mentioned throughout the text that you might want to read. Most of them are in print and can be obtained through the bookstores of New Thought churches or various metaphysical bookstores for retail purchase. All the books, both in and out of print, can be found in most libraries.

A complete listing of books by Dr. Curtis follows. They are all in print and can be ordered retail by individuals, or at wholesale discount by groups and churches from:

Book Department,
Unity Church of Dallas
6525 Forest Lane
Dallas, TX 75230
(214) 233-7106

In addition, albums and tapes of sermons, lectures, lessons, and meditations by Dr. Curtis are available. Please contact Dr. Curtis through the publisher at the following address for a complete listing:

Dr. Donald Curtis
c/o Samuel Weiser Inc.
P.O. Box 612
York Beach, ME 03910

● ● ●

Donald Curtis is the author of over twenty best-selling books in the field of self-improvement, metaphysics, and New Thought. He has traveled widely, studying with the gurus and masters in India, Japan, and other countries. He began his career in the ministry at the Science of Mind Church of Religious Science in Los Angeles. Later he founded the Unity Church of Dallas where, for over twenty years, he was senior minister, conducting classes and seminars on meditation and the human potential. In addition to writing and teaching, Dr. Curtis has been featured on film, television, and radio. He now lives in Desert Hot Springs, California, where he is writing, lecturing, and giving classes on the Ancient Wisdom.